Bloom's BioCritiques

Bloom's BioCritiques

ANTON CHEKHOV

Edited and with an introduction by
Harold Bloom
Sterling Professor of the Humanities
Yale University

CHELSEA HOUSE
PUBLISHERS
An imprint of Infobase Publishing

Bloom's BioCritiques: Anton Chekhov

Chelsea House
An imprint of Infobase Publishing
132 West 31st Street
New York NY 10001

Library of Congress Cataloging-in-Publication Data
Anton Chekhov / edited with an introduction by Harold Bloom.
        p. cm. — (Bloom's biocritiques)
Includes bibliographical references and index.
  ISBN 0-7910-6381-X
  1. Chekhov, Anton Pavlovich, 1860–1904—Criticism and interpretation.
I. Bloom, Harold. II. Series.
  PG3458.Z8 A524 2002
  891.72'3—dc21   2002012916

Chelsea House books are available at special discounts when purchased in bulk quantities for businesses, associations, institutions, or sales promotions. Please call our Special Sales Department in New York at (212) 967-8800 or (800) 322-8755.

You can find Chelsea House on the World Wide Web at
http://www.chelseahouse.com

Contributing editor: Mei Chin
Cover design by Keith Trego
Cover image © Bettman/CORBIS

Printed in the United States of America

Lake EJB 10 9 8 7 6 5 4 3 2

This book is printed on acid-free paper.

CONTENTS

USER'S GUIDE

These volumes are designed to introduce the reader to the life and work of the world's literary masters. Each volume begins with Harold Bloom's essay "The Work in the Writer" and a volume-specific introduction also written by Professor Bloom. Following these unique introductions is an engaging biography that discusses the major life events and important literary accomplishments of the author under consideration.

Furthermore, each volume includes an original critique that not only traces the themes, symbols, and ideas apparent in the author's works, but strives to put those works into a cultural and historical perspective. In addition to the original critique is a brief selection of significant critical essays previously published on the author and his or her works followed by a concise and informative chronology of the writer's life. Finally, each volume concludes with a bibliography of the writer's works, a list of additional readings, and an index of important themes and ideas.

HAROLD BLOOM

The Work in the Writer

Literary biography found its masterpiece in James Boswell's *Life of Samuel Johnson*. Boswell, when he treated Johnson's writings, implicitly commented upon Johnson as found in his work, even as in the great critic's life. Modern instances of literary biography, such as Richard Ellmann's lives of W. B. Yeats, James Joyce, and Oscar Wilde, essentially follow in Boswell's pattern.

That the writer somehow is in the work, we need not doubt, though with William Shakespeare, writer-of-writers, we almost always need to rely upon pure surmise. The exquisite rancidities of the Problem Plays or Dark Comedies seem to express an extraordinary estrangement of Shakespeare from himself. When we read or attend *Troilus and Cressida* and *Measure for Measure*, we may be startled by particular speeches of Ulysses in the first play, or of Vincentio in the second. These speeches, of Ulysses upon hierarchy or upon time, or of Duke Vincentio upon death, are too strong either for their contexts or for the characters of their speakers. The same phenomenon occurs with Parolles, the military impostor of *All's Well That Ends Well*. Utterly disgraced, he nevertheless affirms: "Simply the thing I am/Shall make me live."

In Shakespeare, more even than in his peers, Dante and Cervantes, meaning always starts itself again through excess or overflow. The strongest of Shakespeare's creatures—Falstaff, Hamlet, Iago, Lear, Cleopatra—have an exuberance that is fiercer than their plays can contain. If Ben Jonson was at all correct in his complaint that "Shakespeare wanted art," it could have been only in a sense that he may not have intended. Where do the personalities of Falstaff or Hamlet touch a limit? What was it in Shakespeare that made the two parts of *Henry IV* and *Hamlet* into "plays unlimited"? Neither Falstaff nor Hamlet will be stopped: their wit, their beautiful, laughing speech, their intensity of being—all these are virtually infinite.

In what ways do Falstaff and Hamlet manifest the writer in the work? Evidently, we can never know, or know enough to answer with any authority. But what would happen if we reversed the question, and asked: How did the work form the writer, Shakespeare?

Of Shakespeare's inwardness, his biography tells us nothing. And yet, to an astonishing extent, Shakespeare created our inwardness. At the least, we can speculate that Shakespeare so lived his life as to conceal the depths of his nature, particularly as he rather prematurely aged. We do not have Shakespeare on Shakespeare, as any good reader of the Sonnets comes to realize: they do not constitute a key that unlocks his heart. No sequence of sonnets could be less confessional or more powerfully detached from the poet's self.

The German poet and universal genius, Goethe, affords a superb contrast to Shakespeare. Of Goethe's life, we know more than everything; I wonder sometimes if we know as much about Napoleon or Freud or any other human being who ever has lived, as we know about Goethe. Everywhere, we can find Goethe in his work, so much so that Goethe seems to crowd the writing out, just as Byron and Oscar Wilde seem to usurp their own literary accomplishments. Goethe, cunning beyond measure, nevertheless invested a rival exuberance in his greatest works that could match his personal charisma. The sublime outrageousness of the Second Part of *Faust*, or of the greater lyric and meditative poems, form a Counter-Sublime to Goethe's own daemonic intensity.

Goethe was fascinated by the daemonic in himself; we can doubt that Shakespeare had any such interests. Evidently, Shakespeare abandoned his acting career just before he composed *Measure for Measure* and *Othello*. I surmise that the egregious interventions by Vincentio and Iago displace the actor's energies into a new kind of mischief-making, a fresh opening to a subtler playwriting-within-the-play.

But what had opened Shakespeare to this new awareness? The answer is the work in the writer, *Hamlet* in Shakespeare. One can go further: it was not so much the play, *Hamlet*, as the character Hamlet, who changed Shakespeare's art forever.

Hamlet's personality is so large and varied that it rivals Goethe's own. Ironically Goethe's Faust, his Hamlet, has no personality at all, and is as colorless as Shakespeare himself seems to have chosen to be. Yet nothing could be more colorful than the Second Part of *Faust*, which is peopled by an astonishing array of monsters, grotesque devils, and classical ghosts.

A contrast between Shakespeare and Goethe demonstrates that in each—but in very different ways—we can better find the work in the person, than we can discover that banal entity, the person in the work. Goethe to many of his contemporaries, seemed to be a mortal god. Shakespeare, so far as we know, seemed an affable, rather ordinary fellow, who aged early and became somewhat withdrawn. Yet Faust, though Mephistopheles battles for his soul, is hardly worth the trouble unless you take him as an idea and not as a person. Hamlet is nearly every-idea-in-one, but he is precisely a personality and a person.

Would Hamlet be so astonishingly persuasive if his father's ghost did not haunt him? Falstaff is more alive than Prince Hal, who says that the devil haunts him in the shape of an old fat man. Three years before composing the final *Hamlet*, Shakespeare invented Falstaff, who then never ceased to haunt his creator. Falstaff and Hamlet may be said to best represent the work in the writer, because their influence upon Shakespeare was prodigious. W.H. Auden accurately observed that Falstaff possesses infinite energy: never tired, never bored, and absolutely both witty and happy until Hal's rejection destroys him. Hamlet too has infinite energy, but in him it is more curse than blessing.

Falstaff and Hamlet can be said to occupy the roles in Shakespeare's invented world that Sancho Panza and Don Quixote possess in Cervantes's. Shakespeare's plays from 1610 on (starting with *Twelfth Night*) are thus analogous to the Second Part of Cervantes's epic novel. Sancho and the Don overtly jostle Cervantes for authorship in the Second Part, even as Cervantes battles against the impostor who has pirated a continuation of his work. As a dramatist, Shakespeare manifests the work in the writer more indirectly. Falstaff's prose genius is revived in the scapegoating of Malvolio by Maria and Sir Toby Belch, while Falstaff's darker insights are developed by Feste's melancholic wit. Hamlet's intellectual resourcefulness, already deadly, becomes poisonous in Iago and in Edmund. Yet we have not crossed into the deeper abysses of the work in the writer in later Shakespeare.

No fictive character, before or since, is Falstaff's equal in self-trust. Sir John, whose delight in himself is contagious, has total confidence both in his self-awareness and in the resources of his language. Hamlet, whose self is as strong, and whose language is as copious, nevertheless distrusts both the self and language. Later Shakespeare is, as it were, much under the influence both of Falstaff and of Hamlet, but they tug him in opposite directions. Shakespeare's own copiousness of language is well-nigh incredible: a vocabulary in excess of twenty-one thousand words, almost eighteen hundred of which he coined himself. And of his word-hoard, nearly half are used only once each, as though the perfect setting for each had been found, and need not be repeated. Love for language and faith in language are Falstaffian attributes. Hamlet will darken both that love and that faith in Shakespeare, and perhaps the Sonnets can best be read as Falstaff and Hamlet counterpointing against one another.

Can we surmise how aware Shakespeare was of Falstaff and Hamlet, once they had played themselves into existence? *Henry IV, Part I* appeared in six quarto editions during Shakespeare's lifetime; *Hamlet* possibly had four. Falstaff and Hamlet were played again and again at the Globe, but Shakespeare knew also that they were being read, and he must have had contact with some of those readers. What would it have been like to discuss Falstaff or Hamlet with one of their early readers (presumably also part of their audience at the Globe), if you were the creator of such demiurges? The question would seem nonsensical to most Shakespeare scholars, but then these days they tend to be either ideologues or moldy figs. How can we recover the uncanniness of Falstaff and of Hamlet, when they now have become so familiar?

A writer's influence upon himself is an unexplored problem in criticism, but such an influence is never free from anxieties. The biocritical problem (which this series attempts to explore) can be divided into two areas, difficult to disengage fully. Accomplished works affect the author's life, and also affect her subsequent writings. It is simpler for me to surmise the effect of *Mrs. Dalloway* and *To the Lighthouse* upon Woolf's late *Between the Acts*, than it is to relate Clarissa Dalloway's suicide and Lily Briscoe's capable endurance in art to the tragic death and complex life of Virginia Woolf.

There are writers whose lives were so vivid that they seem sometimes to obscure the literary achievement: Byron, Wilde, Malraux, Hemingway. But most major Western writers do not live that exuberantly, and the greatest of all, Shakespeare, sometimes appears to have adopted the personal mask of colorlessness. And yet there are heroes of literature who struggled titanically with their own eras— Tolstoy, Milton, Victor Hugo—who nevertheless matter more for their works than their lives.

There are great figures—Emily Dickinson, Wallace Stevens, Willa Cather—who seem to have had so little of the full intensity of life when compared to the vitality of their work, that we might almost speak of the work in the work, rather than even of the work in a person. Emily Brontë might well be the extreme instance of such a visionary, surpassing William Blake in that one regard.

I conclude this general introduction to a series of literary bio-critiques by stating a tentative formula or principle for gauging the many ways in which the work influences the person and her subsequent, later work. Our influence upon ourselves is always related to the Shakespearean invention of self-overhearing, which I have written about in several other contexts. Life, as well as poetry and prose, is overheard rather than simply heard. The writer listens to herself as though she were somebody else, and the will to change begins to operate. The forces that live in us include the prior work we have done, and the dreams and waking visions that evade our dismissals.

HAROLD BLOOM

Introduction

1

Anton Chekhov was equally distinguished as short story writer and as dramatist. His influence upon the short story is still ongoing, here in the early twenty-first century. As playwright, he remains almost as influential, though he is now filtered through Beckett and the Absurdists.

Chekhov is so extraordinary a figure, both at storytelling and as theater, that he is best approached obliquely, at some specific angles. Here I will pursue the influences of Chekhov's own work upon his life, as well as the related complexity of Shakespeare's effect upon Chekhov.

Maxim Gorky, the Soviet writer most palpably Chekhov's disciple (and close friend) gives us the best portrait of Chekhov in his wonderful *Recollections*:

> I think that in Anton Chekhov's presence everyone involuntarily felt in himself a desire to be simpler, more truthful, more one's self ...

That is true also of Chekhov's readers, and of the audience at his plays. Setting Shakespeare aside, I can think only of Beckett who is as exemplary and detached a moral influence as Chekhov. Gorky employed Chekhov as his touchstone for authenticity, a role Chekhov's life and work continue to play.

Eric Bentley remarked: "It is as if the theater remembers Chekhov when it remembers its conscience." "Conscience" here mingles aesthetic and transcendental qualities, though there is no transcendence in the honest Chekhov himself. The mystical Lev Shestov, a high transcendentalist, accepts Chekhov's deep inwardness as a secular spirituality, indeed as a "Creation from the Void." Imaginative literature, when it implicitly discourses upon itself, as Chekhov's great plays do, is likely to *sound* religious. Chekhov, a great tragic-comic celebrant of the spirit's necessary self-imprisonment, was not seeking to save anyone, for no one else (since Shakespeare) has seen and shown so well that we cannot be saved from ourselves. Stories and plays cannot make us better.

Chekhov, profoundly under Shakespeare's influence, was particularly obsessed with *Hamlet*. Sometimes, in meditating upon *Hamlet*, I find myself casting Chekhov as Horatio. The first story published under Chekhov's own name, "At Sea," briefly but pungently rewrites *Hamlet*.

The Seagull is a parody of *Hamlet*, but *Uncle Vanya* builds upon Hamlet's own lucidity of consciousness in order to learn the prince's great lesson: questing for the truth, thinking too well, is a dramatic formula for despair. Chekhov, like Hamlet, mourns with antic glee. The unlived life, when your consciousness grasps it, destroys you, with a style of heroic cheerfulness both in Hamlet and in Chekhov. That oxymoronic cheerfulness pragmatically belongs to Shakespeare and to Chekhov, and not to *The Tragedy of Hamlet, Prince of Denmark* and to *Three Sisters* or *The Cherry Orchard*.

2

"I am always in a good mood when I work": if that was Chekhovian irony, it was very gentle. In life, as in art, he was a master of restraint, as Shakespeare was the all-time master of detachment. And yet it is difficult for admirers of Chekhov's plays and stories not to emulate Tolstoy and Gorky: we fall in love with Chekhov, without restraint.

Chekhov's own implicit self-portraits, mostly in the plays, are farcical self-parodies. Shakespeare, so far as I can tell, never once represented himself as a character in his plays. Ben Jonson must have grimaced at Malvolio in *Twelfth Night*, and I wonder how well the ghost of Christopher Marlowe would have tolerated Edmund in *King Lear*. Vershinin, in *Three Sisters*, is Chekhov's masterpiece of self-parody.

3

What was Chekhov's influence upon Chekhov, work upon work, and work upon life? Twenty years before the writer's birth, his grandfather purchased freedom from serfdom. When Chekhov was fifteen, his own bankrupt father departed for Moscow, and the family suffered eviction from their home. The resolute writer became a medical doctor, writing copiously on the side. When Chekhov was twenty-nine, his brother died of the family illness, tuberculosis. Eight years later, the writer received his own death-sentence-to-be, in a similar diagnosis. The years 1897–1904 were immensely productive, though shadowed by what ended Chekhov at forty-four.

How little that life influenced the work! *Uncle Vanya*, *Three Sisters*, *The Cherry Orchard*, and fifty or more great stories are hardly the imaginings of a man who knew he could not reach forty-five, if indeed he got that far. The stories that never leave us are astonishingly varied: "The Kiss," "Rothschild's Fiddle," "The Student," "The Darling," "Gusev," "The Lady with the Dog," "Gooseberries," "The Bishop." They emanate from one another, just as *Three Sisters* and *The Cherry Orchard* emerge from *The Seagull* and *Uncle Vanya*. Something in Chekhov's genius was self-begotten, and flowered by a progressive interiorization, again surprisingly akin to Shakespeare's.

Except for Turgenev, who in *A Sportsman's Sketches* equals him, Chekhov is the supreme short story writer. Except for the great troll, Ibsen, Chekhov is the major Western dramatist since Shakespeare and Molière. Patient and preternaturally modest, Chekhov allowed his astonishing art to shape for him a rather ordinary, sometimes banal life of service to the ill and the poor, to prisoners on Sakhalin Island, and to starving serfs. The superb ironies of the stories and plays produced the counterfigure of the humane Dr. Chekhov, as close to a secular saint as imaginative literature affords us.

ELIZABETH SILVERTHORNE

Biography of Anton Chekhov

UP FROM SLAVERY

"A great wise man, aware of everything,
passed by"
—Maxim Gorky

When Anton Chekhov was 19, he wrote to his youngest brother, Mikhail, scolding him for calling himself 'worthless.' Perhaps, Anton told him, he should feel insignificant before God, Beauty, or Nature— but not before people. "Respect yourself for being a good, honest fellow," he said. "Among people you should be aware of your worth." The idea of the worth of the individual no matter how humble his place in life echoes throughout Chekhov's own life and throughout his writing. It was an idea shaped by suffering and struggle.

Anton Chekhov barely escaped being born into slavery. His grandfather was a serf—a peasant farmer whose master could buy and sell him. Grandfather Egor worked on the estate of Count Chekhov in the heart of Russia, where he made sugar out of beets and fattened cattle on the beet pulp. He then drove the cattle to market and sold them. For his labor he was allowed to keep a small share of the profits.

The word serf comes from the Latin *servus*, which means *slave*. In Europe during the Middle Ages the serfs were on the lowest rung of the social and economic ladder. They were bondsmen, bound to the soil and required to labor for large landowners. These lords of the manors were in turn obliged to provide protection for their serfs.

Most European countries had abolished serfdom by the 1800's, but Russia did not free its serfs until 1861—just as America was beginning the long, bloody Civil War that would result in the freeing of its slaves. For many years there had been violent uprisings and increasing threats of revolt by the Russian serfs. But it was not until Tsar Alexander II warned the nobility, "it is better to abolish serfdom from above than to wait until the serfs begin to liberate themselves from below" that the large landowners seriously began to plan for the emancipation of the serfs.

Prior to these broad-scale changes in the feudal system, serfs with humane masters were sometimes able to buy their freedom. After thirty years of hard labor Grandfather Egor had managed to save up enough money to buy freedom for himself, his wife, and his three sons at 700 rubles a head. One of these sons was Pavel, Anton Chekhov's father.

Anton never forgot that his family evolved from slavery. He worked hard to rid himself of the attitudes and servile feelings that slavery bred. He was determined to live as freely as possible, and, as much as anyone could in the Russia of his time, he lived life on his own terms.

From the time he was a small boy, Anton burned with a spark that nothing could quench. Growing up under the tyranny of a father who beat his children for the slightest offense of word or action only made Anton more compassionate.

The desperate poverty of his childhood only made him more resourceful and hardworking. Constant suffering from poor health and early signs of tuberculosis only made him more determined to live life more fully.

Anton always said that his life was transformed during the three years when he was sixteen to nineteen. During that time he was living on his own, struggling to finish his high school education and having to support himself as well as trying to find ways to help his family, who had fled to Moscow from their hometown of Taganrog. It was during this difficult time that Chekhov realized he had the courage and the energy to control his life.

Years later he also realized he had paid a heavy price for his independence. In a letter to a publisher friend, he admitted that the struggle had cost him his youth, and he summed up his childhood:

Write a story about a young man—the son of a serf, a former grocer, choirboy, schoolboy and university student, raised on respect for rank, kissing the priests' hands, worshiping the ideas of others, and giving thanks for every piece of bread, receiving frequent whippings, making the rounds as a tutor without galoshes, brawling, torturing animals, enjoying dinners at the houses of rich relatives, needlessly hypocritical before God and man merely to acknowledge his own insignificance—write about how this young man squeezes the slave out of himself drop by drop and how, on waking up one fine morning, he finds that the blood coursing through his veins is no longer the blood of a slave, but that of a real human being.

When he was grown, Anton Chekhov loved traveling. Had he been wealthier, he probably would have seen more of the world—as it was, he saw more of the world than many of his contemporaries did. There was a restless spirit in him that urged him to be where he was not. Often when he was in the city, he longed for the peacefulness of the country, and when he was in the country he longed for the excitement of the city. He delighted in being alone in nature and in being in the company of friends whom he constantly urged to visit him wherever he lived—even when it interfered with his work. He loved the company of women and had several brief love affairs but resisted matrimony until very near the end of his life.

Among his friends were famous Russian musicians, artists, and writers of his day: Tchaikovsky, Rachmaninoff, Levitan, Tolstoy, Gorky, and countless other writers, publishers, editors, and common folk. He cherished their friendships and spent countless hours writing long letters to them when they were separated.

After his reputation as an author was established, Chekhov was generous in trying to help aspiring young writers who needed a leg up, but he was honest in his advice and never gave them false praise. He particularly disliked any kind of ceremony in which he was the center of attention and avoided affairs of that kind whenever possible.

Before he was twenty, the family was calling Chekhov "Papa Antosha," and he was for all practical purposes the head of the family from that time on. Instead of leaving home, he assumed the responsibility for creating a home for his parents and siblings.

His training as a scientist influenced his writing in a number of ways. Even though friends scolded him for wasting time chasing after two hares, he continued to practice medicine (usually with little or no remuneration) along with continuing to write until his physical condition absolutely prevented it.

Chekhov's life was short—only forty-four years—yet he produced more literature and crammed more activity into those few years than most people did into lives that were twice as long. His life was full of selfless deeds as well as human failings, and one would suspect that Chekhov wouldn't have had it any other way, for Chekhov was concerned with the human condition. A friend of his once called his stories "funny and heartrending,"—and so they remain over a hundred years after they were originally written.

A Bumpy Childhood

"One beaten boy is worth two unbeaten boys."
—Pavel Chekhov

Taganrog, Anton Chekhov's birthplace, was a prosperous seaport in its early days. Greek ship owners, some of whom had been pirates in other lives, shipped out meat and wheat from the inland areas of Russia. These shipping tycoons founded musical groups and imported French chefs and Italian artists to the city. They also built good schools and large churches.

When the Church of St. Michael was struck by lightning just before Anton's birth on January 17, 1860, his superstitious father was convinced it was a sign of something very good or very evil in the boy's future—it could have been both.

Born Anton Pavlovich Chekhov, he was the third son of Pavel and Evgenia Chekhov. Later, two more brothers and a sister would be added to the family. The Chekhov family moved many times during Anton's early years, sometimes living in rented rooms, but often living with relatives. This crowded, clannish kind of life was common among the small shopkeeper class to which Pavel belonged, and it afforded Anton the opportunity to be close to his extended family—many of whom would show up as characters in his short stories and plays later on.

Pavel Chekhov, who taught himself to play the violin and was a talented painter of holy images, ruled his family like a dictator, proving to be as much a tyrant as any tsar. A fanatical observer of religious rituals and holy days, he believed it was his duty to beat goodness into his children. He made every day fearful for his gentle, inefficient wife and for his children—and for anyone else he felt he had control over. Schoolmates brought home by the Chekhov children soon learned to head for home when Pavel appeared. They knew he might thrash any of them for the most innocent naughtiness.

In a letter to his brother Alexander when they were grown men, Anton recalled his father's behavior. "Despotism and lying so mutilated our childhood that it's sickening and frightening to think about it. Remember the horror and disgust we felt in those times when Father threw a tantrum at dinner over too much salt in the soup and called Mother a fool." Anton warned Alexander against behaving like their father, advising him to be gentle and magnanimous to those in his household who were defenseless.

In many of Anton's stories there are characters based on his memories of his cruel father. In "Three Years" he recalls the anguish he felt as a small child when he has a character say:

> My father began to 'teach' me, or to put it simply, to beat me, when I was less than five years old. He thrashed me with a cane, he boxed my ears, he punched my head and every morning, as I woke up, I wondered, first of all, would I be beaten today?

Pavel was passionately devoted to the Russian Orthodox Church and especially to the sung services. He was the Kapellmeister (choirmaster) of the cathedral choir for three years until he was dismissed for refusing to shorten the unbearably long services he insisted on arranging, despite the congregation's pleas to shorten them.

When he became choirmaster at the Greek monastery, he drafted his three oldest sons, Alexander, Nikolai and Anton, to sing as a trio. After rehearsing them until midnight (and thrashing them when they made mistakes) Pavel hauled them out of bed on freezing mornings for early matins.

Easter was the most important time for the choirmaster, who cared more for the awed reaction of the congregation than for the misery of his three young sons who knelt on icy stones singing through half-frozen lips. For Anton, the result of this early training was that he acquired a dislike of church services and a distrust of religious dogma as expounded by his father. But he also acquired a love for church music and a thorough knowledge of church rituals, which he would also make use of in his writing.

What can be said for Pavel Chekhov is that he wanted his children to have the best education he could afford to give them. During the few years that his general store was showing a profit, he hired a music teacher and a French tutor for them.

As he talked with friends about what kind of education would best prepare his children to lead prosperous lives, he was persuaded by some of his Greek customers that his sons would do well to prepare for jobs in a Greek trading firm. For this they would need to know modern Greek, and so in September of 1867 Anton (age 7) and Nikolai were enrolled in a Greek parish church.

The school was held in one large room where one teacher taught five classes. Older students tested and punished the younger pupils. The red-bearded teacher, Nikolaos Voutzinas, kept order by using his loud voice and metal ruler. In addition to rapping their palms and heads with the ruler, he thought up creative tortures, such as making them kneel on coarse salt, and shaming torments such as the "crucifixion," in which the offending boy was strapped to a stepladder for the class to spit at.

When the year ended and Pavel discovered that Anton and Nikolai had learned nothing more than the Greek alphabet, they were withdrawn from the Greek school and enrolled in the Taganrog *gimnaziya*—a combined grammar and high school. Here Anton would be a student for the next ten years.

In addition to attending school and serving in the church choir, Anton was expected to put in long hours working in his father's store. In the dark and dirty store mingled the aromas of a wide variety of items. On shelves next to coffee, tea, vodka, wine, olive oil, sardines, raisins, sugar, flour, rice, macaroni, lemons, olives, grapes, smoked fish, candies, spices, and sunflower seeds, customers could also find lamp wicks, tallow candles, marbled backing paper for books, penknives, floor polish, mousetraps, brooms, tobacco, leather belts, and a large variety of medicines. For the ladies there were face creams and perfumes. One of the tiresome tasks for the shop boys and the Chekhov sons was to take used tea leaves (bought from hotels), dry them, and repackage them for sale to rich people who bought them for their servants.

There were two shop-boy apprentices aged eleven and twelve years. For the five years of their apprenticeship they were paid no wages and were not allowed to have pockets in their clothing for fear they might steal. Pavel treated them even more harshly than he did his sons, punching and kicking them without mercy until he was called before the Taganrog magistrate for excessive beating.

Although he bowed and scraped toward his customers, encouraging them to linger in his shop over glasses of tea or vodka, Pavel was a poor businessman. As his debts began to mount, he tried opening branch stalls—one by the new railway station and one in the new city market. Along with his brothers, Anton was required to help run these during the summer months. The hours were punishing, as Pavel insisted that the stalls open at five a.m. and stay open until midnight. The returns were meager, however, and the family fortunes were not much improved—if at all.

There were happier moments in Anton's childhood when he and his brothers and friends did the normal things children did for fun in that time and place. In a port city fishing was naturally a favorite pastime, and Smuggler's Bay was a favorite fishing spot for Taganrog boys. Here they caught small, edible Gobius fish that could be sold to the fish market. Chains of these tiny fish, threaded together through the gills, were kept in the water until it was time for the boys to return to the city with their catch. It was here that Anton acquired his lifelong passion for fishing.

Russians often liked to keep finches and other songbirds as pets in their homes, and catching finches in the wasteland proved to be another sport that yielded a few kopecks (100th of a ruble). Probably not as readily saleable were the tarantula spiders Anton caught in the cemetery with a ball of wax.

Escaping the pressures of his home life, work, and lessons to roam the countryside alone or in company gave Anton a wonderful sense of freedom. In his fiction many of his characters also find in nature the same pleasure and escape from their dreary lives.

Anton shared in the schoolboys' mischievous trick of slitting sacks of walnuts in the carts winding their way from the wharf to the town. If the driver caught the young thieves, he struck out at them with his *knout*. This whip (often used on criminals in Russia) ended in leather thongs wired together and hardened by being soaked in a mixture of tar and fish oil. On one occasion the knout struck Anton's trousers with devastating effect. He tried soaking them in chemicals only to have the fabric disintegrate. Fortunately, the mother of a school friend took pity on him and bought him a new pair of trousers, and Pavel never discovered the mishap.

When Anton was eleven, he and his older brother Alexander traveled by ox cart to visit their grandparents, who lived forty-five miles from Taganrog across the steppe—a large tract of treeless land. The journey took two days, and Anton would use many of their experiences sixteen years later in his novelette masterpiece "Steppe." These included being soaked in a storm, getting lost, and encounters with various eccentric people.

As very young children, the boys had enjoyed happy visits to their grandparents, who were working on the estate of a large landowner. But this visit was a terrible disappointment to the brothers when they discovered that Grandfather Egor was hated by the peasants of his village, who called him "the viper." He barely welcomed his grandsons, he ridiculed their schooling, and seemed to take no pleasure in their visit. Their grandmother's spirit was completely broken by her hard life and frequent beatings by her husband. Though the visit was dismal, the brothers more than likely gained some understanding of the harsh childhood their father had suffered, along with some insights into the seeds of his cruelty.

In contrast to both the parish school and home life, the *gimnaziya* was a pleasanter place. There, no physical discipline was allowed, and the only punishment was detention in a small room under the vaulted staircase. There were drawbacks, however, as *gimnaziyas* were under strict government supervision. The tsarist Russian regime was constantly on the watch for any kind of revolutionary ideas, and Russian literature was strictly censored and limited. In its place students were forced to take and pass tough compulsory classical Greek and Latin courses. For Anton and most of the other students, Greek was their biggest hurdle in passing the tests necessary to move up to the next form, or grade.

Some of Anton's teachers remembered him as a clown, who often made the class laugh. He was a leader in devising practical jokes and amusing sayings that the others imitated. He also showed a gift for charming adults as well as the girls whom he met when the girls' and boys' *gimnaziyas* held joint concerts or other entertainments.

When he was thirteen Anton attended the theater for the first time, and he was fascinated by it. Unfortunately, his father, Pavel, believed that the theater was the gateway to hell, and his mother, Evgenia, feared the bad influence of the stage and concert hall. The school was suspicious of the influence of the theater and only allowed the boys to attend authorized plays. As Chekhov discovered, there were ways of getting around the restrictions—doormen could be bribed or school uniforms could be left off. Officially or unofficially, Chekhov managed to attend a large number of vaudeville farces, operettas, and full-length plays. Shakespeare's plays, especially *Hamlet*—which he would write variations on later in life—caught his imagination.

The summer of 1875, when he was fifteen, was the last full summer Chekhov and his brothers would spend together. As often as they could they went to the shore to fish, taking with them a frying pan to cook their catch, and when Pavel was not around, they also took a bottle of Santorini wine.

That same summer Anton had an experience that helped determine his choice of careers. He had been invited by a family acquaintance to spend time on a ranch, and while there he became deathly ill. His hosts rushed him to an inn where the innkeeper and his wife nursed him until he was able to travel. Back home in Taganrog the school physician, Doctor Schrempf, treated Anton for 'peritonitis'. So impressed was Anton with the doctor's skill that he decided medicine would be his life's work.

In the 1870s Pavel's business continued to dwindle. Although people were not then nearly as conscious of safety and hygiene in handling foods as we are today, Pavel's behavior sometimes shocked even his most unsanitary customers. For instance, when he found a dead rat in a barrel of olive oil, instead of pouring the oil out or at least boiling and filtering it, he called in a priest to conduct a service of purification. Word of such behavior predictably lost him even more business.

Finally, Pavel realized something had to be done. He was borrowing more and more money to keep his shelves stocked, but fewer and fewer customers were coming into his store. He gave up the main store and instead focused on trading from the market stalls. When he was unable to pay his dues to the Merchant's Guild, he was expelled. Creditors were threatening to sue; Alexander and Nikolai had gone to Moscow to study, and it was doubtful that the family could pay their fees or even those of Anton's schooling. Extra boarders were taken into the crowded family quarters in Taganrog, but there was seldom enough money to pay for the fuel to heat any rooms other than the kitchen, where they all crowded around the stove to keep from freezing to death.

Pavel had to accept the fact that there was no way he could stay in business in Taganrog. He was being named in at least two lawsuits and was in imminent danger of going to debtor's prison. Before dawn on April 23, 1876, he left town in a cart to avoid his creditors' spies, whom he feared might be looking for him at the railway station. When the cart let him out at a small country station, he boarded a train for Moscow to join his two sons already there.

Three months later, Evgenia followed her husband to Moscow, taking with her the two youngest children, Mariya and Mikhail. The money for their fares came from what Anton was able to raise by selling household goods and from tutoring fellow students. At sixteen Anton was burdened with responsibility for his own survival and often for that of the rest of his family.

MEDICAL STUDENT AND COMIC WRITER

"All my hope lies in the future."
—Chekhov to Dmitry Grigorovich

Although he was on his own at 16, Anton's life was far from carefree. Pavel could not find work in Moscow—or at least not a job he could hold on to for more than a day or two. A barrage of letters from both parents pressured Anton to raise money by selling pieces of furniture, finding tenants for the Taganrog house, and collecting some small debts owed Pavel. The three rubles a week Anton earned by tutoring barely covered his expenses. He had to live with relatives, take meals with them, and even beg postage stamps from them.

The winter of 1876-77 was severely cold and dismal. Pavel wrote whining letters urging Anton to work harder and send more rubles. He declared that he had always been an affectionate, self-sacrificing father, and now he expected support from his sons. Anton's mother complained, "We've had 2 letters from you full of jokes while we had only 4 kopecks for bread and dripping and waited for you to send money .... We sleep on the floor in a cold room." What she failed to understand was that for her son, humor was the means by which he could fight despair. Anton took on more students and sent more of his hard-earned money to Moscow.

During the Easter holiday of 1877, Chekhov made his first trip to Moscow, where he spent two weeks with his family. Their living conditions dismayed him—in a furnished room, heated by the wood Nikolai stole, the entire family lay down to sleep each night on a single mattress. Mariya, now fourteen, cleaned, cooked, washed, and knitted wool shawls to sell for a few kopecks apiece; Evgenia woke before dawn to work at the sewing she took in; Alexander was involved in an affair with a married woman and spent the little money he earned on her; and Nikolai spent more time at the local tavern than at the School of Fine Arts where he was supposed to be studying.

However, the city itself was exciting to Chekhov. He enjoyed roaming the streets with his brothers, but more importantly, his twenty-five-year-old cousin Misha, with whom he formed a strong friendship, took him to the theater. After he returned to Taganrog, Anton wrote to Misha asking him to continue to comfort Evgenia. "She is physically and morally crushed, and has found in you much more than merely a nephew," he told him.

During the four years he was in high school (1876-1879) Chekhov spent his summer holidays on the ranch of a Cossack friend. Here he rode horses bareback and went hunting to supply meat for the dinner table. He also joined the young men of the family in spying on peasant girls as they bathed in a pond, and one day he kissed one of them by the well.

Literature was not considered very important at the *gimnaziya*, and the books on the library shelves were strictly censored lest they should cause the students to have radical ideas. Fortunately for Chekhov, he discovered the public library, where he could read works by Shakespeare and Cervantes. At times he had to withdraw his reading membership fee for a while in order to buy food, but he always restored it as quickly as possible. He often wrote to his younger brothers trying to impress them with the joy of reading the classics.

As Anton neared the end of his final semester, his parents wrote to say that they could hardly wait for him to come to Moscow, and that they were not pleased with his brothers' behavior. Alexander, the oldest, earned little money by teaching and selling an occasional short article to a humor magazine, while Nikolai, a talented artist, sometimes sold a painting or a drawing for the cover of a magazine. But Pavel was dismayed that the boys spent the little money they earned on clothes, liquor, and women rather than helping the family.

But before he could graduate from the *gimnaziya* Chekhov had to pass a series of grueling examinations that began on May 15 and lasted for almost a month. If he failed any of these exams, he would be subject to military service and would not be allowed to enter the university. The first exam was the 'Russian Essay' on the topic "There is no greater evil than anarchy." Chekhov wrote for nearly six hours and received a commendation for his literary style. In the following days he earned "5's" (the highest mark) for Scripture, Religious Knowledge, Geography, French and German. His marks in Latin, Greek, mathematics, physics, natural science, and Russian language and literature were qualifying "4's" and "3's"—good enough to earn a matriculation certificate.

Ready to make the move to Moscow, Chekhov applied for the official government permission that allowed citizens to move from town to town. While he waited for his official papers to be prepared, Chekhov kept busy. He lobbied the Taganrog city council for a fellowship paying 25 silver rubles a month—and he won it. He also talked the mothers of two students who were going to the university into letting their sons board with the Chekhovs. They would each pay 20 rubles per month, which would prove a big help to Evgenia in managing the household. Finally on August 6, 1879, Chekhov boarded the train for Moscow—his 'ticket to leave' described Chekhov as being 6'1" with dark auburn hair and eyebrows and black eyes (actually they were brown). Pictures of him taken as a young man (before tuberculosis caused drastic changes in his appearance) all show that he was quite handsome.

He received a warm welcome, and immediately found himself in the role of head of the family—a role he would play for the rest of his life. The family's circumstances improved at once. His cheerfulness lifted the daily gloom, and his practical help lifted the financial pressure. Pavel, who finally had a lowly job at a Moscow warehouse, some distance away, often spent the night there, and Anton's two older brothers,

Alexander and Nikolai, were living their own lives away from home. The three younger children and his mother were happy to have Anton as the principal breadwinner and one responsible for the welfare of the family.

As head of the household, one of Chekhov's first decisions was to move the family from the dark basement apartment that they had occupied to lighter, roomier living quarters. He also persuaded his mother to stop buying food in bulk on credit and instead to buy with cash what was needed at the time. Under Anton's management no longer did she have to take in washing, and no longer did his sister Mariya have to hire herself out as a cook in other people's homes.

In 1879, Chekhov registered at the Medical Department of the University of Moscow, which had a reputation as a first-class school. Classes were held in clinics, and 200 students graduated annually from a demanding five-year course. On the faculty were outstanding professors, some of them world-renowned. First-year students, however, were taught by junior assistants.

Chekhov's tough schedule included inorganic chemistry, physics, botany, zoology, mineralogy, and theology. In anatomy class each student had his own corpse to dissect. The bodies often came from the poor of Moscow—criminals who had been hanged, victims of starvation or disease or accidents, or people who had died of old age with no kin or friends to bury them. Dissection of corpses was good training in observation and analysis, and Chekhov developed skills that led to his becoming known for accurate diagnoses of his patients' diseases when he became a practicing physician.

Socially, he had a gift for making and keeping friends. Some of his teachers and fellow students would remain in close contact with him for the remainder of his life. His brother Nikolai introduced him to art students who also became life-long friends—including Frans Schechtel, who would design the cover for Anton's first collection of short stories, and Isaak Levitan, who would become Russia's leading landscape painter. After their years at school, and until Levitan's death from tuberculosis, Chekhov and Levitan often visited with each other, helped each other with their work, and sometimes proved friendly rivals for the affection of the same woman.

Life in Moscow was expensive, and Chekhov was eager to increase the family's income even while he was struggling to keep up with his studies. Understanding that Alexander and Nikolai had found a way to earn a little money by selling stories and cartoons to cheap humor magazines such as *Dragonfly* and *Alarm Clock*, Chekhov too decided to try this approach.

While he was at the *gimnaziya* in Taganrog, Chekhov had started a handwritten class magazine, *The Stammerer*, and he, as well as other young people in Taganrog, enjoyed the satirical magazines published in Moscow and St. Petersburg. These resembled the popular United States' *Mad* magazine in their zany humor that poked fun at pompous people and stuffy ideas.

Within months of beginning medical school, Chekhov was submitting stories and sketches to Moscow's weekly humor magazines. Rejections only made him try again, and on December 24, 1877, the *Dragonfly* published his short sketch, "Letter to a Learned Neighbor." The main characters in the story were caricatures of his bullying grandfather and father.

Chekhov soon became a prolific contributor of humorous sketches and stories to the humor magazines—such contributions usually sold for ten to twenty kopecks. The rates were low, and it was necessary to write a great deal to make even a little money. He often wrote under different pen names for different magazines, using "Antosha Chekhonte," a nickname his favorite teacher of religion had given him in Taganrog.

Chekhov had no delusions that he was writing great literature, and he knew that the potboilers he wrote to keep his family fed and himself in medical school required speed. He considered medicine his profession and writing to be the work that helped pay for his learning of it. Much of what he wrote at that time has not survived—he himself destroyed some of his early writings, calling it "piffle."

However, since his death as a revered and famous author, unending attempts have been made to find and reprint even his most trivial work. Two early short novels written during his time at the university were revived after his death and actually made into movies. The first, *Useless Victory*, was made into two Russian silent films, while the murder mystery *The Shooting Party* was made into a Hollywood movie called *Summer Storm*.

Chekhov's first summer vacation must have come as a great relief from the strenuous mental activities of studying and writing. He spent a month with his fellow medical student Vasili, who was one of the young men he had recruited as a boarder with the Chekhovs in Moscow. At

Vasili's home in the steppes, the two friends kept in practice by dissecting rats and frogs. Visiting Taganrog on his way back to Moscow, Chekhov picked up a human skull to decorate his room. He may have gotten it from the old Quarantine cemetery where as a young boy he had hunted skulls with other Taganrog urchins.

Second-year medical studies were demanding; students were required to dissect corpses by day and study pharmacology by night. Then in March shocking events at the highest government level distracted the students, and much of the Russian populace. In the middle of St. Petersburg, Tsar Alexander II was assassinated by a terrorist's bomb. Known as the "Tsar Liberator" for his role in freeing the serfs, Alexander II made enlightened reforms in education and government restrictions, but the new Tsar, Alexander III, set about reversing his father's liberal policies. He tightened governmental control over the daily living of the people, setting off protests and public dissent.

Chekhov attended some of the protest meetings on the campus, but was not as active a rebel as some of his friends who found themselves jailed for their beliefs. However, once the new regime began persecuting minorities, Chekhov assured his Jewish friends of his loyalty and support. One of the lasting effects of the new regime on Chekhov's writing career was the increased censorship that banned any cartoons or writing that contained the least bit of criticism of the government.

Third-year medical students at the university worked on live patients. New courses included: diagnostics, obstetrics, gynecology, and venereal diseases. During this year Chekhov's earnings from his writing increased when he became a regular contributor to a new weekly Moscow magazine, *The Spectator*. Also connected with the magazine were three of his brothers: Alexander as an editorial secretary, Nikolai as an artist, and the youngest, Mikhail, as an occasional translator and tea boy.

By now Chekhov had amassed a huge pile of published sketches and stories, and in an effort to increase his earnings, he compiled a book of 160 pages of what he considered his best work—employing Nikolai to illustrate it. But even though the stories had passed censorship once (when they appeared in magazines), the more repressive censors of the new rule banned the book when it was in page proof. For Chekhov, this meant writing at an even faster pace for the low-paying magazines in order to earn enough money to support the family.

Chekhov's last two years as a medical student and writer demanded superhuman effort. The outstanding professors for whom the university was noted now taught his classes, and their expectations of the about-to-be doctors were high.

It was also at this time that he realized that many people considered Moscow magazines frivolous, and that to be recognized as a writer, one had to appear in St. Petersburg magazines. Thus, when an opportunity opened for Chekhov to write a column for the St. Petersburg weekly *Fragments*, he accepted it. His column, called "Fragments from Moscow," included current events such as trials, scandals, and the latest stage shows. Covering these events proved to be good training as a journalist.

The conditions under which he often had to work would have forced less tenacious writers to resign, and in August of 1883 he wrote to the editor of *Fragments*: "I'm writing under abominable conditions. Before me sits my nonliterary work pummeling mercilessly away at my conscience. The fledgling of a visiting kinsman is screaming in the room next door, and in another room my father is reading aloud to my mother ... Someone has wound up the music box, and I can hear *La Belle Helene* ...."

Pavel, who earned very little to help the family, complained that Anton was burning too many candles by writing late at night. Furthermore, Alexander and Nikolai were wasting their time and talents by heavy drinking and running up debts. As usual, it was up to Anton to keep the family afloat.

Although he didn't think of himself as a serious writer, years of constant scribbling had taught him a great deal about the craft of writing. Toward the end of 1883 he published a short story, "He Understood," in *Nature and Field* magazine, using his real name for the first time. Editors were beginning to recognize the talent of the prolific writer whose work appeared under different names in many magazines.

Final exams for the graduating class of the medical school began in the winter of 1883-84, in which the students had to undergo a stiff course assessment by their demanding professors and also pass a total of 75 examinations. One of Chekhov's tests was to do an autopsy on a man who had committed suicide while intoxicated—an experience he would later use as the germ for several short stories.

On June 16, 1884, Dr. Anton Chekhov received a certificate designating him as a General Practitioner of Medicine. In addition to certifying that he was qualified to practice medicine, it meant he was not subject to military service and did not have to pay poll tax. After this he displayed a sign advertising his readiness to see patients.

DOCTOR AND SERIOUS WRITER

> *"Medicine is my lawful wife;*
> *Writing is my mistress."*
> —Anton Chekhov

The brass nameplate on their door reading "Dr. A. P. Chekhov" delighted Pavel and Evgenia, who were tremendously proud of having a son with the title of doctor. They felt sure he would soon be earning fat fees, and the family would be lifted out of its perpetual poverty.

Their dependence on Anton was greater than ever as his older brothers were contributing little to nothing to the family income. Alexander barely made enough money as a customs worker to support his common-law wife and baby. He drank heavily and lacked the discipline to utilize his writing talents. Nikolai, also a heavy drinker, accrued debts and then disappeared, leaving Anton to deal with his creditors. Worse yet, on a visit to brother Vanya's school, Nikolai played silly tricks that displeased the authorities and got Vanya fired from his teaching job. Anton, who called Vanya the "solid" brother and was proud of his dependability, was disgusted. He loved his older brothers, but there was little he could do to control their behavior.

Doctor Chekhov soon discovered that medicine was not the road to riches his parents expected. House calls paid five rubles, which barely paid for the upkeep of the horse and carriage necessary to make them. Most of his patients were so poor they often paid him with homemade goods or promises. And many of his friends expected him to treat them and their servants for free, presuming on their friendship as sufficient pay.

Being called out to see patients at any time of the day or night during the bitterly cold Moscow winter took its toll on Chekhov's own health. He was often exhausted and began to spit up blood when he coughed. He told friends it was only a blood vessel in his throat that had burst. But he was an exceptionally good diagnostician and of course was aware that many of his relatives had tuberculosis—reason enough for alarm at this symptom.

Tuberculosis, also known as the white plague, was widespread in Russia in the nineteenth century—as it was in most of Europe. No effective drugs had yet been discovered to treat it. Its contagiousness was not generally appreciated, although Robert Koch, a German physician, announced in 1882 the discovery of *tubercle bacilli* and demonstrated that it was, in fact, an infectious disease. It *had* been proven that patients who rested, ate nutritious diets, and avoided cold, damp climates were apt to do better than those who did not. However, this was not a regimen the busy young doctor and writer was willing to follow.

Because his payment for the short stories that appeared in the comic magazines was low, he had to continue writing at a hastened pace in order to earn enough money to meet the family's basic needs. Chekhov advised another aspiring writer: "Write as much as you can!! Write, write, write till your fingers break!" He, himself, certainly lived by this motto. Like Dickens, who roamed the streets of London absorbing the sights, sounds, and smells, Chekhov roamed through Moscow's markets, taverns and brothels in search of atmosphere for stories. He also experienced in person the seedier side of life in the city—carousing in the taverns with friends and visiting houses of prostitution.

At the age of 26 Chekhov found himself frequently attending the weddings of doctor friends and joining in the wild celebrations that followed the solemn ceremonies. Physically exhausted from too much celebrating, he began to think he needed a wife to steady him. He formed friendships and had love affairs with some of the attractive young women his sister Mariya brought home, and even became secretly engaged to one of them, Dunya Efros, a Jewess.

Chekhov did not share the widespread anti-Semitism of his day. Several of his short stories dating from the time of this liaison (especially "Mire") explore the feelings of sensitive Russian Jews to the discrimination and repression they lived under. However, he was not ready for marriage, and the engagement was broken. It would be another 15 years before he finally married, during which time he and Dunya remained friends—she eventually outlived him and died in a concentration camp in 1943 at the age of 80.

Although he did not admit the seriousness of his illness, Chekhov knew he needed a vacation from the hectic pace of his life in Moscow. In accordance, when an opportunity to rent a cottage cheaply on a land-owner's estate at Babkino (about 30 miles from Moscow) arose, he moved the family there. For a nature lover like Chekhov it was a paradise. There were gardens and hothouses, a splendid forest, and perhaps best of all, there was a river with excellent fishing.

He had a room to himself where he could write in the mornings. The afternoons he usually spent fishing. One of his best stories from this time is based on a legend he had heard from the locals about a huge fish; the title is "The Burbot," sometimes translated as "The Fish." In the evenings he happily joined in the parties at the landowner's mansion, where there might have been charades, music, and impromptu skits. Sometimes he earned a little extra income by covering for the local doctor. For the next three years the family escaped in the summers to the pleasures of Babkino.

In the relaxed atmosphere of Babkino Chekhov began to write longer and better stories. These began appearing in the "thick" St. Petersburg journals, which were considered more respectable than the cheap comic magazines where so much of his early work appeared. His work began to catch the attention of critics and other recognized writers. A major breakthrough in his writing career occurred when Alexei Suvorin accepted some of his stories for Suvorin's St. Petersburg newspaper New Times.

This acceptance also marked the beginning of one of the most important friendships in Chekhov's life. While the giants of the golden age of Russian literature in the nineteenth century—Pushkin, Tolstoy, Turgenev, and Dostoevsky—all came from the nobility, and their paths as writers were relatively smooth, Suvorin and Chekhov shared the same background in that they had struggled up from peasant ancestry.

By the time they met, Suvorin (who was 26 years older than Chekhov) had risen from extreme poverty to become a millionaire. In addition to owning New Times, he was a book publisher and a bookseller with a monopoly on the book stands at all of the Russian railroad stations, and he had tried his hand at writing novels, essays, and plays. At the beginning of their friendship, Suvorin was Chekhov's mentor, offering useful advice about his writing and persuading him to use his real name as his byline. As time went by it was often Chekhov who gave Suvorin advice.

Because *New Times* was considered ultra conservative, some of Chekhov's friends were afraid his writing would be restricted by its policies. The freedom-loving young writer had no intention of allowing this to happen, and he resisted Suvorin's request that he write exclusively for *New Times*. Despite differences in some of their beliefs, the friendship proved to be mutually helpful and satisfying over many years. It also came to include members of both their families.

One of their shared interests was the legitimate stage. From the time Chekhov saw his first theatrical performances as a schoolboy in Taganrog, he was enchanted by the stage. While he was still in high school he began experimenting with playwriting, and while he was in medical school he wrote a long, sprawling melodrama without a name. Realizing it was not producible he put it away, but bits and pieces from its themes and characters can be traced in his mature plays.

In the late 1880's Chekhov wrote several quite successful one-act plays that were popularly known as vaudevilles. Today one of these, "The Bear" (sometimes called "The Brute" or "The Boor") appears frequently in American high school and college anthologies. Although Chekhov referred to these as "shabby, stupid vaudevilles" and expressed amazement at their popularity, he was happy to get the income from their performances.

Ivanov, Chekhov's first four-act play to be performed in Moscow, was written at the request of Fyodor Korsh, who owned a theater in the city. Chekhov wrote the play in less than two weeks, but by the time he sat down to write it he had been a student of the theater for more than a decade and had very definite ideas about plays and playwrights.

When one of his editor friends advised him to keep out of the way while the play was in production, Chekhov told him:

(1) the play is the author's property, not the actors'
(2) where the author is present, casting the play is his responsibility
(3) *all* my comments to date have improved the production
(4) the actors themselves ask for my comments
(5) if you reduce author participation to naught, what the hell will you come up with?

The ten rehearsals Korsh promised were reduced to four, and despite his hands-on approach Chekhov was disappointed with the opening night performance. He described the premiere with his usual humor to his brother Alexander, telling him that it caused more excitement than the prompter had seen in all his 32 years with the theater. "People were screaming and yelling and clapping and hissing, there was almost a brawl in the buffet, some students in the gallery tried to throw someone out and two people were ejected by the police," he told him. Despite the fact that some of the actors were drunk and didn't get a single line right, there were numerous curtain calls after each act.

Reviews by newspaper critics were mixed. Comments by reviewers and friends convinced Chekhov that *Ivanov* was misunderstood, and he planned serious revisions before it opened in St. Petersburg. In that city it was also successful although the actors treated it as melodrama, and it was popular for the wrong reasons according to Chekhov's thinking.

Chekhov wanted to change the way conventional Russian drama was presented. He wanted to get away from the traditional hero-villain roles and stock plots, and he wanted the things that happened onstage to be as they were in real life—"just as complex and just as simple." On the surface people might be sitting around having tea or a meal, but at the same time "their happiness is being created or their lives are being smashed up." He eventually achieved his aims and made a lasting impact on the ways plays are written and presented not only in Russia but also throughout the western world. When a friend predicted that he would write better plays than *Ivanov* in the future, Chekhov agreed. It would, however, take a few years.

Chekhov's family circle, he told a friend, "tied him hand and foot." His Moscow household now consisted of his mother and father, Mikhail (still a student), Nikolai (who spent his time drinking and lying about), Mariya, Vanya (who was teaching), and his aunt Fenicka and her son. He sent Mikhail to hunt for a place where the family could spend the summer of 1888. Pavel and Evgenia wanted to go to the Ukraine where they had grown up. By luck Mikhail found rooms in the wing of an old mansion on an estate called Luka near the Ukrainian town of Sumy on the river Psyol.

The Chekhovs and the Lintvaryov family, owners of the estate, soon became close friends. Chekhov was pleased to discover that the widowed matriarch of the family was an avid reader and admirer of artists and writers as well as an avid fisherman. He marveled at the happy spirit of the oldest daughter, a physician, who had a brain tumor, was blind, and suffered constant headaches and yet laughed, joked, and enjoyed listening to his stories read aloud. He went with the second daughter, also a physician, to visit her patients at the local clinic. He described her to Suvorin as "a quiet, shy, infinitely kind and loving, homely creature." The third daughter "muscular, suntanned and raucous" had built a school on the estate at her own expense and taught there. The two sons he found untalented but honest and hardworking.

The river was wide and deep with an abundance of islands, fish, and crayfish. Nightingales sang day and night, lime trees were in flower, and blooming jasmine scented the air. Wandering the overgrown gardens and seeing the boarded-up manors, he felt he had fallen into an enchanted fairy tale. Every day he took a boat to the sixteen-wheel water mill "complete with a miller and his daughter." In the evenings he rowed over to the islands to fish with the fishing addicts from the factory, and sometimes went with them on all-night fishing expeditions. Inconveniences, such as the lack of inside plumbing and the fact that the Lintvaryovs were so outspokenly liberal that they were under government surveillance and Chekhov's own mail was being censored, were easy to overlook in such an idyllic setting.

As usual, Chekhov's two incorrigible older brothers caused trouble even in paradise. Soon after Alexander arrived, he went to Sumy where he got drunk and tried to assist a local conjuror and hypnotist who was performing at the little theater in the public park. Alexander had to be dragged from the stage protesting and swearing. Back at Luka he wrote a letter proposing marriage to the Lintvaryovs' second daughter. Elena. Chekhov destroyed the letter, and after a terrific row, Alexander left for Moscow.

Shortly after this Nikolai arrived in disgrace. He had been helping the architect and family friend Franz Schechtel restore a church in Moscow when one day he took Schechtel's money and materials and vanished, only to surface at the Luka estate. Nikolai was suffering from advanced tuberculosis, which his alcoholism only made worse, and he was gaining a reputation as an unreliable artist. Chekhov was glad to escape for a while by accepting Suvorin's invitation to visit his villa at Feodosia in the Crimea. There the friends swam, sunbathed, strolled, and talked literature for nine days.

By the fall of 1888, Suvorin had published three collections of Chekhov's short stories. Now he went to work lobbying the Imperial

Academy of Sciences to nominate Chekhov's last volume, *In The Twilight*, for the Pushkin Prize for literature. Chekhov won and received the award of 500 rubles. Notice of the award brought him recognition in literary circles and numerous petitions by aspiring young writers for advice. His response was always to be as helpful as possible if he saw the least possibility in their writing.

Back in his noisy Moscow setting that fall and winter Chekhov worked on *The Wood Demon*, a play he and Suvorin had discussed at length in Feodosia. It was destined to be a failure, closing after only three performances at a small Moscow theater. It had a theme expressing Chekhov's strong feeling of the need for conservation, but it was too long and too dense. Parts of it, however, were later incorporated into his successful play *Uncle Vanya*.

The following summer the Chekhov menagerie returned to Sumy, but this time they were not in holiday mood as Nikolai was extremely ill. Chekhov, who had been his doctor and his nurse since the middle of March, diagnosed typhoid fever as well as tuberculosis. He sent Evgenia and Mikhail ahead to prepare their rooms at the Luka estate, and then took Nikolai by first class sleeping car to Sumy. There Nikolai lay in a hammock coughing incessantly. When Suvorin came for a six-day visit, Nikolai asked him for an advance for book cover designs—which Chekhov forbade Suvorin to pay.

By June Nikolai was bedridden, emaciated, and sometimes delirious. Chekhov stayed in the adjoining room. Exhausted from months of caretaking, he planned a short visit to friends about 100 miles away. No sooner had he arrived at his destination than a telegram reached him saying that Nikolai had died in Alexander's arms. He returned to Luka in time to take part in the traditional Ukrainian funeral that the Lintvaryovs arranged, which included having the Chekhov brothers carry Nikolai's body in an open coffin to the cemetery.

Following Nikolai's death Chekhov fell into a state of restlessness and depression. He sought distraction by taking a number of short trips and by burying himself in his writing. From this period dates "A Dreary Story," one of his most powerful short stories. The protagonist is a professor of medicine with an incurable disease who knows he will die of it but has not told his family. Clearly Nikolai's death made Chekhov mindful of his own mortality.

To Suvorin Chekhov wrote: "There's not a kopeck's worth of poetry left in life."

However, he never gave in to melancholy for very long. If life was short and uncertain, it could be risked in search of adventure and a worthy cause. And so as the decade ended Chekhov was planning a long, grueling trip across Siberia. His friends were appalled.

JOURNEY TO THE HEART OF DARKNESS

"The island seems to me a perfect hell."
—Anton Chekhov

The name Siberia comes from a Tatar word meaning "sleeping land." It's a vast land about one and two-thirds times as large as the United States. Lying in northern Asia, it is bordered by the Artic Ocean, the Bering Sea, The Pacific Ocean, the Ural Mountains, and China. During the long winters the temperature falls lower than it does at the North Pole, and in the short summers the average temperature is only between 50 and 65°F.

Chekhov's destination was the Imperial Russian penal colony on the island of Sakhalin located off the eastern edge of Siberia, nearly 6,000 miles from Moscow.

The famous trans-Siberian railroad would not even be started until the year after his trip, and it would not be completed until the year after his death.

Most Russians considered Siberia as a place to be avoided—a notorious, isolated land where hardened criminals and political exiles were sent. It was certainly not considered a desirable destination for a normal traveler in his right mind. Chekhov's family and friends were horrified at the idea of his making such a hazardous trip alone and not in the best of health (he had been coughing up blood that winter). Evgenia was sure the trip would kill him.

Suvorin told him his duty was to literature and not to investigative reporting. At first he refused to help him with his research or to use his influence with government authorities to gain permission for Chekhov to visit the penal colony. Only after Chekhov convinced him that he was determined to go did Suvorin relent. Perhaps at first it was an impulsive wish to do something to shake off the depression and sadness he felt after Nikolai's death, combined with his natural restlessness, that made the potentially dangerous adventure appeal to him, but the more he read about conditions in Siberia, the more he began to see the journey as an opportunity to expose some terrible wrongs.

In a letter to Suvorin, Chekhov explained (as much as he ever explained) his reasons for going to Siberia. He expected, he said, to write at least 100 to 200 pages about the conditions there from a scientific standpoint. Since he had not written the usual dissertation at the end of his medical studies, he felt this would "pay off" his debt to medicine. He anticipated the journey would mean six months of continuous physical and mental labor, which he said he "absolutely" needed, as he was a Southerner and had begun to grow lazy. He knew he might be hardheaded and capricious in his determination to go, but what, he asked his friend, did he have to lose: "Time? Money? My time is worth nothing, and I never have any money anyway."

He was indignant with Suvorin for saying that Sakhalin could be of no use or interest to anyone:

> Sakhalin can be useless and uninteresting only to a society which does not exile thousands of people to it.... we have sent *millions* of men to rot in prison, have destroyed them— casually without thinking, barbarously.... have depraved them, have multiplied criminals, and the blame for all this we have thrown upon the gaolers and red-nosed super- intendents. Now all educated Europe knows that it is not the superintendents that are to blame, but all of us....

Chekhov did his homework before leaving. He got his sister Mariya and his brother Alexander to look up hundreds of references for him in St. Petersburg libraries and archives. Suvorin supplied books, references and letters, and other friends let him use their personal libraries. At last, in late April he set off accompanied by Mariya and friends on the first leg of his journey. His equipment included an army officer's waterproof leather coat, top boots, a revolver, and a long knife for "cutting sausages and hunting tigers."

From then on he endured a rough, lonely journey. May of 1890 turned out to be the coldest May in Siberia in forty years. He often gave thanks for his thick leather coat that protected him from hypothermia and from broken bones in the jolting he received in unsprung carts on deeply rutted roads. Nevertheless, his shoulders and back ached so much for the first 1,000 miles that he couldn't stand, sit, or lie in comfort, and he sat "like a goldfinch in a cage" in a hired basketwork chaise.

Snow finally gave way to heavy rain and gales. Mud and floods often left him bogged down or stranded for days, and he almost drowned crossing the River Tom.

Finally he hired his own cart and driver, hoping to make better time, but his circumstances were hardly improved. At each washed-out crossing or broken bridge he or the driver had to get out and lead each of the horses across separately. On one occasion Evgenia's prophecy that he would be killed almost came true when he was involved in a crash. He described the accident in a letter to a friend:

> Suddenly I see a troika heading for us at full speed; my driver turns right in the very nick of time and the troika dashes past us.... It is followed by another coach also going at full speed. We turn to the right, it turns to the left. "We'll collide!" flashes through my mind. Another instant, and there is a crash, the horses tangle in a black mass, my carriage rears up and I am on the ground with all my bags and bundles on top of me. I jump up and see: a third troika bearing down on us!

He and his driver managed to jump out of the way, but the cart was damaged, the harness torn, the shafts were broken, and the yokes lying about in the road. He discovered the drivers of the second and third troikas had been asleep. In the darkness, in the middle of the wreckage and the cursing, frenzied drivers, he was overcome "by a sense of utter loneliness such as I have never known before."

Vodka was always plentiful in Siberia, but food was sometimes scarce and frequently unappealing. He thought the "brick tea" tasted like a mixture of sage and beetles, and the muddy duck soup and fish cooked with the scales on were "disgusting." He often subsisted on bread and pancakes, and when he did get a good meal of cabbage soup with meat and roast potatoes he was ecstatic.

When he reached Irkutsk, the capital of Siberia, he stayed for a week. He took his first bath and threw away his filthy clothes and bought new ones. By the time he reached the Amur River, it was June and the weather was warm enough to swim during their stops at villages along the way. After all of the hardships he had endured, he was delighted to be on a steamship on the river. "I've fallen in love with the Amur," he wrote to Suvorin. "It's beautiful and spacious and free and warm.... The lowliest convict on the Amur breathes more freely than the highest-placed general in Russia."

Russia was on his left and China on his right. He had a friendly curiosity about other nationalities and took every opportunity to get to know them. He reported to Suvorin that the Chinese were "awfully polite, very ceremonial, well dressed, and eat delicious food."

At some of the stops he kept up his medical practice, treating the local people, including gold prospectors and their families. Everywhere in Siberia he heard talk of "gold, gold, gold." What could be more interesting, he asked Suvorin, than chatting and dining with gold smugglers?

On July 5th, after two and a half months of traveling, he arrived at Nikolayevsk, the port of embarkation for the island of Sakhalin. Among the passengers making the crossing were a number of prisoners. One he saw was accompanied by his five-year-old daughter, who clung to his shackles as they came up the gangway.

Chekhov's first sight of Sakhalin might well have been a glimpse of Hades. Monstrous fires were burning, and as far as he could see, flames, smoke, and fiery sparks lit the black sky, outlining the silhouettes of mountains. It seemed to him the entire island was on fire.

He was to spend three months in this "perfect hell." Chilly rain, fog, and vicious mosquitoes made life miserable even in the short arctic summer. The officials were cordial and cooperative, although Chekhov quickly discovered they were apparently unaware of (or unwilling to acknowledge) the barbarities he learned about soon after his arrival. These included daily floggings, embezzlement of food and medicine, and violence against the natives, including murder.

He encountered no opposition to his plan of taking a complete census of the entire population of the island, and he was allowed to have 10,000 survey cards printed in the print shop. On these questionnaires he wanted to gather information the Russian government had not bothered to collect. In addition to name, address, age, place of birth, and religion, the cards asked questions about year of arrival, trade, literacy, source of income, married state, and diseases.

In an amazing physical effort he covered every settlement on the island, stopping at each hut to collect information. He told Suvorin, "There's not a single convict or settler on Sakhalin who hasn't talked with me." He was especially pleased with his children's census and had hopes he could do something to improve their lot. He convinced the local officials to order textbooks from Suvorin, and telegraphed his brother Vanya to send books and school programs.

The children played a game called soldiers-and-convicts and accepted as a fact of life that their fathers or mothers might be murderers. He found that the children loved their "impure mothers and criminal fathers more than anything else in the world." He understood the children were often the only tie that bound their parents to life and saved them from despair, but he could not understand how the parents could be indifferent to child prostitution, which was common.

There were twice as many men as women in the penal colony, as well as a number of "bachelor soldiers." So when news of the arrival of a new group of women convicts spread, the road leading to the port of arrival was jammed with prospective bridegrooms or "suitors" as they were called. Chekhov recorded the mating game:

> When they arrive at the post they are permitted to enter the women's barracks and they are left there with the women. The suitors wander around the plank beds, silently and seriously eyeing the women; the latter sit with downcast eyes. Each man makes his choice. Without grimaces, without any sneers, very seriously, they act with humanity toward the ugly, the old and those with criminal features..... If some younger or older woman "reveals herself" to a man, he sits down beside her and begins a sincere conversation. She asks if he owns a samovar and whether his hut is covered with planks or straw.... Only after the housekeeping examination has been completed, when both feel that a deal has been made, does she venture to say: "You won't hurt me in any way, will you?" The couple then leaves together to his home and become "cohabitants."

Chekhov noted that most of the women convicts were sentenced for crimes of passion. When a woman told him: "I came because of my husband" or "I came because of my mother-in-law," it usually meant she had murdered that person.

Other than jailers or other prisoners, Chekhov was the only Russian most of the exiles had seen since their deportation. He was always a sympathetic listener, and during their interviews they talked and often wept. Sometimes he helped them with their medical problems, and on one occasion he bought a heifer for a family.

As a trained physician Chekhov put aside his revulsion as he observed and took notes on the human degradation he witnessed. Seeing convicts chained to wheelbarrows and hearing the clang of iron as gangs of shackled men marched to work were everyday experiences. He forced himself to witness a flogging, but after a few strokes by the sadistic beater had turned the naked back of the victim into a bloody mass of raw flesh, he had to flee the scene. As a compassionate man he was deeply affected by all that he saw and told Suvorin he felt "a bitterness in my innards."

He found some relief in studying nature—the forests, animals, birds, and fish as well as the few crops that grew in the unfriendly soil. When he studied the few hundred aborigines, Gilyaks and Ainu, who survived on fish and berries, he discovered their numbers had been greatly reduced by diseases brought to the island by Japanese and Russian invaders. Also, escaped convicts and renegade guards plundered the little they had and treated them brutally.

On October 6 he wrote to his mother: "I'm homesick and weary of Sakhalin. For three months I've seen no one but convicts or people who can talk of nothing but penal servitude, the lash, or jailbirds. It is a depressing existence." He planned to return home by sea. The voyage would take two months, and there would be some uneasy moments.

Conditions in the maritime region on the east coast, including Vladivostok, from which he embarked, dismayed him. He felt despair over the poverty, ignorance, and pettiness that characterized the people. "For every honest man there are ninety-nine thieves who are a disgrace to the Russian people," he said.

His steamship, *The Petersburg*, had to bypass Japan because cholera was raging there. Their first port of call was Hong Kong, which pleased Chekhov greatly. He praised the "marvelous" bay and the excellent roads. He rode in a jinrikisha and bought lots of souvenirs. When fellow passengers criticized the British colonials for exploiting the Chinese, he thought of what he had just seen of Russian colonization of the natives on Sakhalin. He agreed that the English exploited the Chinese and Hindus, but in return "gives them roads, water mains, museums, and Christianity. You [Russians] do your own exploiting, but what do you give in return?"

When in the South China Sea, a typhoon overtook the ship. During heavy gales it keeled over as far as 38 degrees, and disaster seemed imminent. The captain advised Chekhov to keep his loaded revolver handy, as he thought being shot preferable to being drowned. Fortunately, they weathered the storm, and Chekhov didn't have to make that choice.

Watching two burials at sea unnerved Chekhov. Seeing a corpse wrapped in sailcloth somersault into the ocean, he was filled with horror at the realization that it was several miles to the bottom. However, the experience eventually resulted in a fine short story, "Gusev," about a burial at sea. With his writer's imagination he added a terrifying detail. At the end of the story a shark stealthily approaches the sinking canvas shroud containing the body of Gusev and begins to rip it open.

Chekhov called Ceylon (now Sri Lanka) "a paradise of palm trees and bronze-skinned women," and he enjoyed their time in India where he saw wild elephants and cobras and bought two mongooses. These small furry animals provided much entertainment for Chekhov and the other passengers during the long days when there was little else to do but look at the sea.

When they received a telegram saying the *Petersburg* had arrived at Odessa and Chekhov was boarding a train for Moscow, Evgenia and Mikhail hurried to Tula (about four hours from Moscow) to greet him and accompany him on the last leg of his trip. They found him at the station restaurant with two friends he had picked up along the way. One of the mongooses was sitting on the table eating with them, and a small crowd had gathered to watch.

His family was delighted at his safe return. In his absence they had moved to a new house, where Pavel had marked his son's travels on a large wall map. Suvorin had taken the family under his wing in Chekhov's absence, but they had sorely missed his leadership during the almost eight months he had been gone.

The day after his return he sat down to write to Suvorin. He told his friend that the trip had changed his thinking about many things:

"God's world is good. Only one thing in it is bad: we ourselves." Russians have no sense of justice, he said. "What is needed is work, and the hell with everything else."

A. CHEKHOV, LANDOWNER

> *"Being lord of the manor is quite nice."*
> —Anton Chekhov

Chekhov was anxious to get started on his book exposing the conditions on Sakhalin. But the trip had been expensive, so his first priority was to write short fiction to earn enough rubles to keep the family going. It wasn't easy: the small house was crowded, it was hard to find time and space to concentrate on writing, and he was suffering from influenza.

The mongooses proved to be a happy distraction. They were, he told a friend, "very cheerful, lively beasts." They were daring, affectionate and extremely curious. When a stranger appeared they poked around in his pockets to see what they could find, and they opened every package that arrived. Pavel, however, did not find them so amusing when they leaped on the table and broke dishes, dug up pot plants, and bit the twitching toes of sleeping guests.

In January, Chekhov went to St. Petersburg for a three-week visit with the Suvorins. He had many friends there now and was soon caught up in a round of partying and drinking until he exhausted both himself and his hosts. Many women were attracted to the handsome, popular writer. He enjoyed their attention and flirted with them and teased them, but he resisted getting involved in any serious relationships.

In between his social activities, Chekhov lobbied influential people on behalf of the children of Sakhalin. Eventually he helped arrange for orphanages to be set up there for 120 of the child beggars and prostitutes. Furthermore, thanks to his persistence, several thousand books were sent to the island.

On his return to Moscow, Chekhov shuffled his piles of paper on Sakhalin and tried to settle down. But his restlessness increased daily. When Suvorin suggested a grand tour of Europe, Chekhov jumped at the chance. His family was dismayed. To go on a long trip so soon after being away for eight months! And what about money? Mariya accused him of being "fidgety." But Chekhov wouldn't hear their complaints. He felt it was an opportunity that might not come again. "My soul is leaping with delight," he wrote Suvorin. On March 17 they left, along with Suvorin's oldest son, Alexei Jr., for Vienna.

This trip was a stark contrast to his journey through Siberia. Looking around his luxurious train compartment furnished with beds, mirrors, rugs, and huge windows, he remembered the broken-down carriages in which he'd jolted over the atrocious roads to reach Sakhalin.

Vienna delighted Chekhov. He wrote to his family praising the architecture, the churches, the boulevards, the monuments, and the bookstores down every side street. Compared to Moscow, everything— including the women and the restaurants—was so elegant. The shops, with their marvelous art objects, made his head spin. He always had a weakness for neckties, and he wrote, "Take ties alone, there are billions of them!" But perhaps most impressive of all was the realization that people could publish, read, write, and speak freely without the fear of government restriction or punishment.

Venice was even more enchanting than Vienna. At night, gliding in a gondola along the canals, Chekhov watched other boats hung with lanterns and listened to the music of guitars, violins, mandolins, and voices. Memories of the hot, brilliant sunshine and the sounds of tolling bells and the "sensation of complete and utter freedom" would be described in "An Anonymous Story" several years later.

Heavy rains dampened his enthusiasm for other cities in Italy— Bologna, Florence, and Rome. He grew tired of plodding through the Vatican and museums and art galleries and of eating rich foreign food. His feet and his back ached, and he was hungry for good Russian cabbage soup and buckwheat porridge. The beauty of Naples Bay revived his spirits, although he found the streets of the city "filthy."

April 4 found the travelers in Pompeii. After imbibing a large quantity of the local red wine, he rode horseback to the foot of Vesuvius and then struggled up the side of the volcano on foot. He sent Mariya a description of the three and a half hour climb and the crater:

> What a torture it is to climb Vesuvius! Ashes, mountains of lava, congealed waves of molten minerals, mounds and all sorts of nasty things. You take one step forward and fall a half step back. The soles of your feet hurt; you have trouble

breathing.... The earth surrounding it [the crater] is covered with a thin coating of sulphur and gives off a dense vapor. A noxious white smoke pours out of the crater, sparks and red-hot rocks fly everywhere, Satan lies snoring beneath the smoke. There is a mixture of sounds: you hear thunder clapping, railroad trains pounding, boards falling. It is all quite terrifying, and at the same time makes you want to jump right down into the maw. I now believe in Hell.

They then moved on to France, staying in Nice and Paris. Chekhov and Alexei Jr. went to Monte Carlo to gamble at roulette. After losing on the first day, Chekhov worked out a system he was sure couldn't lose. For a while his pockets bulged with his winnings. "Never before had I seen so much gold and silver," he told Mariya. But by the end of the day he didn't have a franc left. He was unrepentant. He knew the family would be justified in saying, "We're living in poverty and he plays roulette." He agreed, "That's perfectly just, and I give you permission to slit my throat." But he was pleased to have experienced the sensations felt by gambling addicts. After all, everything was grist for the writer's mill.

At Easter time he was in Paris, missing being with his family and participating in all the Russian traditions connected with this important church season. The French were a "wonderful" people and the Eiffel Tower a marvel, but he was homesick and eagerly looking forward to getting back to work. Finally, on May 2, after six weeks abroad, they returned to Russia.

Chekhov badly needed to get to work. Traveling with Suvorin meant going first class all the way, and he was heavily in debt. Pavel had quit his low-paying job, and Chekhov needed to find a place for the family where he could have room to work. In a small village a short distance from Moscow, he rented the ground floor of a large house with spacious grounds and a pond stocked with fish.

Here he began a grueling work schedule. On Monday, Tuesday, and Wednesday he worked on the Sakhalin book; on Thursday, Friday, and Saturday he worked on his long short story "The Duel," and on Sunday he wrote shorter short stories. Up at four or five in the morning, he made coffee and began writing. At eleven he went fishing or mushrooming. After lunch and a short nap, he went back to work. There were usually guests for dinner and talk in the evening.

Levitan, the painter, came for a long stay as did the beautiful Lika, Mariya's friend, who was in love with Chekhov. He enjoyed her company but resisted her attempts to lure him into marriage. Medicine was yet another distraction from his writing. When the local peasants discovered a doctor had come to stay, they lined up for treatment, which he willingly gave for little or no pay. By the end of the summer, Chekhov had finished "The Duel" and made some progress on the Sakhalin book, although he told Suvorin it had become hard labor.

In the winter of 1891-92 much of Russia was famine-stricken following a severe drought, and Chekhov devoted most of that winter to famine relief work. During this time, he discovered a practical way to help that did not involve simply giving handouts to starving peasants. He worked with a friend to raise funds to buy the horses of peasants (who were slaughtering them for food), fatten the horses during the winter, and then give them back to the peasants in time for spring planting. During the fund-raising campaign, he told Suvorin he had become a good "beggar."

Chekhov was growing increasingly disgusted with the confined living quarters of his house in Moscow. If the family could live in a comfortable home in the country, he thought he would find freedom to write and also achieve better health. When he heard that a house and grounds near the village of Melikhovo was available (two and a half hours from Moscow by train), he eagerly entered into negotiations for it. The cost was staggering, 13,000 rubles, but it was an estate such as the "son of a serf" had dreamed of owning. Along with the house were nearly 600 acres of land, including a park, a garden, some woodland, and a long avenue of lime trees. The outbuildings included barns, sheds, and a poultry house. Best of all there was a pond that could be stocked with fish. Chekhov borrowed the down payment from Suvorin and got a ten-year mortgage for the rest.

The family soon discovered that a lot of repairs would be needed to make the place livable. Before they could move in, they had to dispossess swarms of bedbugs, beetles, cockroaches, and mice. Chekhov, who hated killing animals, trapped the mice and set them free in the woods. Fortunately, labor was cheap in the country. Carpenters, painters, cleaners, and farm laborers were hired to work along with the family to repair sheds and fences, erect partitions, add a bathroom, dig a new well, and rebuild all of the tile stoves.

The family worked harder than the hired help, rising at dawn and going to bed soon after dark. The move delighted old Pavel. The former serf took on the airs of a grand aristocratic landowner, insisting the servants call him "master," and organizing the music program at the church in Melikhovo. Evgenia managed the housework with the help of a cook and maid, and provided abundant meals for the family and soon for numerous visitors. Mariya worked long hours in the large vegetable garden, wearing a kerchief over her head and heavy men's boots on her feet. The youngest brother, Mikhail, proved to be a natural farm manager—rising early to direct the field workers, and supervising the plowing and planting. By May, oats, clover, grasses, potatoes, lentils, peas, and buckwheat were all planted.

Chekhov, who loved trees and flowers passionately, took as his assignment the care of the orchard and flower garden. That first spring he planted eighty apple and sixty cherry trees as well as lilacs and roses and other flowers. Since he said that all he knew about farming was that dirt was black, he pored over agricultural books and wrote to experts for advice. He enjoyed hoeing, digging, weeding, planting, and transplanting. As he lopped off dead branches and chopped down dead trees, he developed bulging muscles. Friends sent gifts of seeds, bulbs, and plants as well as horses and poultry.

By summer the place was in good shape. The house had been renovated, with floors re-laid and painting and wallpapering finished. The enlarged pond was stocked with a huge variety of fish. A croquet lawn was ready. There were mountains of cucumbers and cabbages, more gooseberries than they could pick, and luscious cherries and strawberries.

The hospitable and gregarious Chekhov could not resist urging relations and friends to visit, and they came, sometimes in over-whelming numbers, so that beds had to be set up all over the house. While the constant stream of visitors entertained him, they also exhausted him and kept him from his work. Chekhov solved that problem by building a little lodge for himself away from the house where he would not be disturbed in his writing.

Mariya, as always, fiercely protected his privacy. During his lifetime his attractive sister received a number of proposals of marriage, but her devotion to Chekhov and his growing dependence on her made her refuse them all. Her unconditional loving care also may have made bachelorhood more appealing to him than marriage with its inevitable demands. During this time, Chekhov continued his ever more intruding medical practice, and while he sometimes rebelled (in letters to friends) against being called out at all times of day and night in all kinds of weather, he never refused an urgent summons from neighbors and local villagers. Sometimes he was called out four or five times in a day. If a workman was injured, a baby scalded, or a pregnant woman faced a difficult delivery, the peasants soon learned that Dr. Chekhov would not refuse to help. Treatments and medicine were free, although sometimes he would be given a pig or gifts of food by grateful patients.

When cholera began creeping toward Melikhovo, Chekhov abandoned his writing entirely and spent his time helping prepare for the expected epidemic. He was appointed a sanitary inspector and doctor for his district, which included twenty-five villages, four factories, and a monastery. Traveling from village to village giving lectures on how to avoid contamination, treating patients, arranging for isolation shelters with space for future patients, and struggling with authorities to obtain supplies exhausted him. "I'm poor and broke," he told Alexei Suvorin, "because I thought it desirable for myself and my independence to refuse the remuneration cholera doctors receive." But he was proud of the fact that his district was prepared to curtail the number of deaths from the disease, despite the fact that the peasants to whom he lectured were "unsanitary and mistrustful." Thanks partly to his tenacity, cholera stopped short of his district, and with the coming of cold weather the threat of an epidemic gradually faded.

With the onset of winter weather, Chekhov's spirits dropped. The cold, white silence, snow-covered fields and bare trees, long nights, and days without sun depressed him. He made trips to Moscow and St. Petersburg and dreamed of traveling to foreign lands. He enjoyed planning a spring trip to the Chicago 1893 Columbian Exposition with a son of Tolstoy. Eventually he withdrew from the trip because of the expense, but another underlying reason was his health. He had palpitations of the heart, was coughing blood, and suffered from excruciatingly painful hemorrhoids. Being confined to the house with his parents meant enduring daily the constant religious blathering of his father (for whom he felt only a sense of duty) and listening to the platitudes of his simple-minded mother, whom he loved, but who could never understand his brilliant mind.

He managed to write some short stories during the long, frozen months. He also enjoyed having time for reading—especially the famous Russian authors, Turgenev and Tolstoy. He wrote to Suvorin that he found Turgenev "delightful, but much weaker than Tolstoy." Comparing Turgenev's women characters to Tolstoy's Anna Karenina, he found most of them "so much nonsense."

In the winter, travel was entirely by sled, but with the spring thaw and rains, the roads turned to mud, often making it impossible to get into town by any means. Finally, toward the end of April the cold spring relented, and Chekhov was once again able to take walks through the fields and warm himself in the sun. His constant companions were two dachshunds, Bromide and Quinine, gifts from a friend. They trotted along with him whether he was walking or horseback riding, and they slept in his bedroom.

During the summer of 1893 Chekhov spent much time making preparations against another threatened invasion of cholera and treating "a thousand patients." He also worked sporadically on his cumbersome book on Sakhalin, and planted more trees and welcomed a stream of visitors—joining them in fishing, picnicking, hiking, and evening entertainments. But, as many friends who recorded their memories of him commented, there was a remoteness and sometimes a sense of underlying sadness underneath his constant joking and playfulness.

As usual, several young women were in love with him. He enjoyed and encouraged their adoration and attention, flirting with and teasing them, calling them his "squadron" and himself their "admiral." However, when any relationship came dangerously close to matrimony, he hastily backed away, leaving more than one woman in a state of helpless frustration.

By 1894 *The Island of Sakhalin* began to appear serially in the journal *Russian Thought*. It appeared in book form in 1895—after four years of hard work, several revisions, and bouts with the censors. The book was a mixture of painfully gathered statistics and dramatic revelations of life in the penal colony. According to his creed of telling the whole truth, Chekhov tried hard to be just. For instance, in writing about the aborigine Gilyaks, he says they are clever, intelligent, cheerful, brash, and not afraid of authority. But he also describes their attitude toward their women, who can be sold or kicked out of the house. They sometimes pet their dogs, he says, but never their women.

Chekhov was careful not to pass judgment on the morality of the prisoners as he revealed their activities. They resorted to deceit and thievery, he said, because experience had proven to them that deceit was the best and most dependable strategy in the struggle for existence. They stole from each other in the prison; they stole from settlers, and at their work when loading ships "with the tenacity and avarice of hungry locusts." He told of the extensive gambling and vodka drinking that served as subversive amusements, and of the prostitution that included the selling of young girls. He described the callous behavior of prison officials and the shrieks of prisoners who were being mercilessly beaten.

The Island of Sakhalin was widely and favorably reviewed by the Russian press. Prison experts in Russia studied the book, and eventually the government was pressured to bring about certain reforms in the treatment of the convicts and in their living conditions. Chekhov was relieved to have finished this self-imposed task, and felt he had at last paid a debt he owed to medicine.

It's interesting to note that Sakhalin has again come into the news as the 21st century begins. The discovery of rich deposits of oil has made it home to the largest foreign investment projects in Russia. Chekhov would no doubt be fascinated by the prospect that this place that he equated with hell could become the means by which Russia raises itself out of its economic depression.

THE TOLSTOYAN IMPACT

> *"I have loved no man as I have loved him."*
> —Anton Chekhov

In 1895 Chekhov finally met Leo Tolstoy, Russia's grand old man of letters. When Tolstoy's epic *War and Peace* stunned the literary world with its brilliance, Anton Chekhov was still a small child, and he was only fifteen when Tolstoy's great love story *Anna Karenina* was published. As a young man Chekhov read and reread these masterpieces with a feeling of awe for such a talent. Like all educated Russians he knew the fascinating story of this wealthy aristocrat who had tried to lead the life of a simple peasant.

Count Leo Tolstoy was born in 1828 into Russian nobility on the large family estate of Yasnaya Polyana, about 100 miles from Moscow. Impatient with the teaching at the university he was attending, Tolstoy returned to the family home at the age of nineteen to educate himself. Bored with country life, he began sowing his wild oats in Moscow and St. Petersburg—carousing in nightclubs, drinking heavily, and womanizing. Finally, disgusted with this useless existence, he joined the army in 1851 and was honored for bravery while fighting in the Crimean War.

Upon his return to Yasnaya Polyana, he decided to educate the peasantry. He built a school and taught there himself, using original teaching methods with considerable success. He also wrote and published textbooks to make learning easier. In 1862 he married an intelligent girl from a middle-class family. Eventually they had thirteen children. With the publication of *War and Peace* and *Anna Karenina* he achieved recognition as a writer of genius.

Although he was the wealthy owner of a large estate, happily married, and a famous writer, Tolstoy was deeply unhappy. He spent years searching for the purpose of life. Finally he decided the answer lay in the teachings of Christ as revealed in the New Testament: the purpose of our lives is to do good. He rejected the authority of the church and of the government. He condemned private ownership of property and wanted to give all of his estate to peasants—until his family persuaded him to legally transfer it to them. In his effort to live as simply as possible, Tolstoy gave up tobacco and alcohol and became a vegetarian. He wore a simple peasant's smock and worked in the fields with the peasants, made his own boots, and cleaned his own room.

Denouncing his earlier writings, Tolstoy used his extraordinary persuasive powers in books, pamphlets, and articles expounding his ideas of the moral life. As a result, he soon had a large following of people who became known as "disciples of Tolstoy." While in his twenties, Chekhov, too, fell under Tolstoy's spell, and for six or seven years Tolstoy's thinking governed his life. He was, he later said, almost hypnotized by the way Tolstoy expressed his ideas.

Chekhov didn't feel the need, however, to imitate Tolstoy's life style by trying to live like a peasant, and he certainly didn't share Tolstoy's scorn of doctors, medicine, or scientific progress. But he was deeply in accord with the idea of doing good, and it was Tolstoy's response to the famine crisis in 1891 that had stirred Chekhov into action. When it became evident the government was trying to hide the facts from the public, Tolstoy wrote articles revealing the tragedy, both for the Russian people and for people abroad. He also organized hundreds of food kitchens sustaining 9,000 peasants and raised 140,000 rubles for famine relief. Taking note of all this, Chekhov wrote to Suvorin, "Tolstoy—ah, that Tolstoy! In these days he is not a man but a superman, a Jupiter."

As Chekhov matured in his writing and in his thinking, he emerged from Tolstoy's spell. In 1894 Chekhov told Suvorin, "Somehow or other, Tolstoy has passed out of my life." This was hardly true, for even as Chekhov rejected Tolstoy the prophet, he was about to embrace Tolstoy the man in a strong and lasting friendship.

By 1895 literary critics were linking the names of Chekhov and Tolstoy and calling them the two most important living Russian writers. Friends reported to Chekhov that Tolstoy had praised some of his stories and even attempted to call on him in Moscow, at a time when Chekhov was absent from the city. It was time, he decided, to meet the sage of Yasnaya Polyana.

On August 8 they met on a tree-lined path leading to the river that ran through the estate. Tolstoy, dressed in a white smock with a towel over his shoulder, was on his way to bathe in the river. He invited Chekhov to join him, and together they undressed and jumped in the water. Here, naked, neck deep in water, they had their first face-to-face conversation. Chekhov enjoyed the humor of the situation and described it in his notebook and to friends.

That evening there was a reading of Tolstoy's work-in-progress, *Resurrection*. Chekhov made a suggestion based on his knowledge of the penal code from the time he had spent in Siberia; he pointed out that the sentence handed down to one of the characters was too light. Tolstoy accepted his advice and made the correction. Chekhov already knew one of Tolstoy's sons. Now, meeting the daughters for the first time, he found them charming, and their obvious adoration of their father increased his respect for Tolstoy.

After that first meeting, their friendship grew steadily deeper—despite the thirty-two-year age gap and despite their very different ideas on some subjects. Tolstoy's main concern was with men's spiritual health rather than their bodily welfare, which was Chekhov's deep concern.

Chekhov believed that technological advances—railways, telegraphs, telephones, electricity, and steam—would improve the lives of all people, while Tolstoy thought these things were unimportant and even undesirable. Chekhov was detached and skeptical about religion, whereas Tolstoy was a passionate believer. Tolstoy believed he had found the truth, while Chekhov believed we can only search for the truth, but can never be sure of having found it.

While he rejected Tolstoy's more extreme ideas, Chekhov had great admiration for his influence for good. Once, when Tolstoy was reported to be seriously ill, Chekhov wrote to a friend, "Tolstoy's moral influence is so great, that there are people who are ashamed to do evil things simply because Tolstoy lives."

Although the two writers had great appreciation for each other's writing talent, they freely criticized what they did not like. Chekhov complained of the excessive moralizing in some of Tolstoy's later works and of his occasional tendency to write about things he didn't know about and hadn't bothered to research. Tolstoy had high praise for many of Chekhov's short stories and thought the short vaudeville skit *The Bear* very amusing. But he disliked Chekhov's long plays—an idea Chekhov found highly amusing, since Tolstoy had told him he detested Shakespeare's plays.

On January 28, 1900, Chekhov wrote to Mikhail Menshikov, a well-known journalist, expressing his feelings about Tolstoy:

> First, I have loved no man as I have loved him. I am not a believer, but of all beliefs I consider his the closest to mine and most suitable for me. Second, when literature has a Tolstoy, it is easy and gratifying to be a writer....Third, Tolstoy stands above us, his authority is enormous.... If not for him, literature would be a flock without a shepherd or an unfathomable jumble.

Each year, with the coming of warm weather, life at Melikhovo was full and satisfying. From a neglected, run-down estate Chekhov had created a charming retreat. His orchard and forest were thriving, and he had become an expert at growing flowers. Hyacinths, columbines, zinnias, asters, and many varieties of roses beautified the grounds. Being close to nature, digging in the earth, fishing, mushrooming, and tramping through the fields with Bromide and Quinine at his heels soothed Chekhov's spirits. Although the mongooses amused guests by demonstrating their snake-catching ability, they became a little too wild and were consigned to the Moscow Zoo, where Mariya sometimes visited them.

In addition to running a free clinic for the peasants in the Melikhovo area, Chekhov became deeply involved in community affairs. Where he saw a need he worked until it was met. Often this meant putting aside his own needs for time to write and time to rest and conserve his strength. And often it meant using his powers of persuasion to twist arms as well as digging into his own pockets to supply funds. As a result of his efforts, the community acquired a new firehouse, a postal and telegraph station, a new highway, a rebuilt bridge, and a new church cupola with a large glass cross that reflected sunlight and moonlight.

Like Tolstoy, Chekhov believed that ignorance was the main cause of the sufferings of the large peasant class and that good schools were the cure. A major contribution on his part was the building of three schools in the area. He was shocked at the condition of the old school at Talezh, a neighboring village. The living conditions of the teacher and students horrified him, and he arranged for daily hot meals to be served to them. Then he went to work to build a new school.

Whatever had to be done, he did. After overcoming the objections of local authorities and supporters of the wretched parochial school, he raised funds by organizing amateur concerts and plays, extracting contributions from well-off local citizens and far-away friends, and using his own money. Fascinated, as always, by building anything, he himself designed the building. He planned a light, airy structure with lots of windows. He ordered all of the materials, down to the tiles, and he supervised the carpenters, bricklayers, and plumbers in their work.

When they saw what he had accomplished, the district board thanked him for his efforts. At the formal opening of the school, grateful villagers presented him with an icon, silver salt-cellars, and loaves of bread—traditional peasant symbols of hospitality and appreciation.

Chekhov was proud that the school was the finest in the area, but he was annoyed with the newspapers that mentioned his name in connection with it. All he wanted in exchange for his efforts, he said, was love. At about this same time he was collecting and buying large quantities of books for the library in his old hometown of Taganrog. His one request was that the gifts be given in strict anonymity. Eventually

Chekhov built two more schools—one in another neighboring hamlet and another at Melikhovo village. Again he was financier, architect, and work supervisor.

Despite the never-ending distractions of country life, Chekhov managed to find time to write some of his best stories and one of his best plays while living at Melikhovo between 1892 and 1898. The long story "Peasants" caused a huge outburst of excitement and controversy. As a physician Chekhov had treated thousands of peasants and visited hundreds of their crude dwellings. Always a keen observer, he knew what living on the edge of starvation did to them and to their relationships with each other. In "Peasants" he gives a vivid picture of the harshness and brutality of their lives. He shows men drowning in vodka, women beaten like animals, and children, filthy and hungry, becoming coarsened under grinding poverty and neglect.

This close-up of the Russian peasant class was far different from the idealized view that Tolstoy and many others held. They preferred to believe that under the peasants' grimy smocks beat hearts of gold, and that they lived together in peace and mutual cooperation. The government of the Russian empire was greatly disturbed by Chekhov's stark revelations. When the story was first printed, censors chopped out some of the more offensive paragraphs. However, Suvorin (whose pro-government leaning gained him favors) managed to publish the entire story before the year was out.

The reaction was astounding. Numerous reviews praised Chekhov for shedding light on a terribly dark situation. Others called him the Russian equivalent of a blaspheming liar. Letters of congratulations and of condemnation poured in from friends and strangers. Although Chekhov, as always, refused to get involved in politics, followers of Karl Marx used "Peasants" to promote their expanding communistic crusade.

At the beginning of 1897 Russia conducted a census. During January and February Chekhov was deeply involved in the strenuous business of counting people and recording economic information in Melikhovo and neighboring villages in the hope that it might lead to improvements in living conditions for the peasants of the area. On his birthday, January 17, he wrote to Suvorin to say he was so terribly busy he couldn't take time to visit St. Petersburg. "I've never had as much work as I do now," he told him. But in March, an event occurred that forced a temporary halt to his hectic schedule.

For at least ten years Chekhov had suffered symptoms of tuberculosis—racking coughing spells, night sweats, palpitations, and coughing of blood. Despite the urging of family and friends, he had consistently refused to be checked by another doctor, hiding his symptoms or denying they could be anything serious.

On March 22 he met Suvorin for dinner at the Hermitage, one of Moscow's most elegant restaurants. During the first course, as Chekhov opened his mouth to speak, a torrent of blood gushed out and he collapsed. He suffered more hemorrhages over the next two days and was finally persuaded to be hospitalized. At the clinic where he was taken, advanced tuberculosis affecting both lungs was diagnosed.

Tolstoy visited Chekhov at the clinic, ignoring the ten-minute visiting rule and exhausting him with a long harangue on immortality. During Chekhov's two-week stay at the clinic, a constant stream of visitors interrupted his rest. They were let in two at a time, and after telling Chekhov not to try to talk, kept asking him questions. He also felt obliged to answer personally the large number of letters he received from well-wishers.

Convalescence at Melikhovo was not much more restful. The same swarm of visitors arrived, and now they had to be offered hospitality. His doctors ordered Chekhov to change his way of life, and he reluctantly agreed to follow some of their advice. He gave up liquor and tried to eat more nourishing foods. He also gave up practicing medicine on a regular basis. But it was harder to say no to requests for his help with civic affairs, and as soon as he had enough energy he was again involved in fund-raising projects for the schools in the area.

The doctors' main restriction was that he not spend his winters in the harsh climate of central Russia. Accordingly, Chekhov went to Nice, France, in September of 1897 and stayed in France for eight months. The boardinghouse where he lodged was a haven for visiting Russians, and the landlady was noted for serving good Russian dishes like borscht. He read a great deal but found it hard to write at a strange desk in foreign surroundings. He turned out about a dozen stories in all and brushed up his French by taking lessons. He took some side trips—to Biarritz to visit friends and to Monte Carlo to gamble. He had a number of visitors from Russia and tried to lure Suvorin to Nice, telling him: "The weather is warm and very pleasant. Sitting on the embankment, basking in the sun and looking out to sea is sheer delight."

Mariya struggled to manage Melikhovo and keep their parents happy. Chekhov sent her instructions about the garden and reminded her to give a ruble at Christmas to the cowherd, three rubles to the village priest, and small gifts to the children at the schools. He arranged to have flowers delivered to his mother for the holidays.

The last few weeks of his trip were spent in Paris with Suvorin. While he waited anxiously for word from Mariya that the weather was warm enough for him to return to Melikhovo, Chekhov shopped for gifts for the family. He arranged for a sculptor to carve a twenty-foot statue of Peter the Great for the 200th anniversary celebration of his hometown, Taganrog, and he purchased 300 books by classical French writers for the Taganrog library.

On May 2 he took the Nord-Express train from Paris for St. Petersburg, and on May 5 he was in Melikhovo. His father wrote in his diary: "Antosha has returned from France. He has brought back many gifts." His mother wrote to Mikhail: "He arrived at five in the evening. He has lost a lot of weight."

"DEAR ACTRESS"

"Hello, last page of my life...."
—Anton Chekhov

Chekhov spent the summer of 1898 at Melikhovo gardening, working on community projects, writing, entertaining visitors, and strolling around the estate followed by Bromide, Quinine, and a brown cow. As fall approached and the weather turned cold and damp, his doctors advised him to go south, and he left for Yalta in the Crimea. At that time Yalta was already a popular seaside resort, and even the Tsar had a winter palace nearby.

In October Pavel died following an operation for a rupture. Chekhov knew his mother and Mariya could not manage the estate on their own, and he never questioned that it was his responsibility to provide a home for them. He also knew that for the rest of his life he would have to spend the cold months—which amounted to the greater part of the year—in a warmer climate. Reluctantly he put Melikhovo up for sale and purchased land in Autka, a village that was a few minutes' walk from Yalta. Soon he was eagerly involved in plans to build a house with an orchard, flowerbeds, and a vegetable garden. He planned to grow even better roses than those he was famous for at Melikhovo. There were several kinds of mushrooms in the area, so Evgenia could enjoy her favorite hobby of mushroom gathering.

Chekhov never managed money very well. When he had it, he spent it and gave it away generously to charities and individuals in need. Now in his need for immediate funds he made a serious mistake. Upon Tolstoy's recommendation he went to Adolph Marx, a new publisher, who had a reputation for sharp dealing. After some negotiating, Chekhov sold Marx outright all the copyrights on his works—past, present, and future—with the exception of copyrights to his plays. The result was that Marx eventually made a fortune at Chekhov's expense, and Chekhov was never free from money worries.

The contract was for 75,000 rubles, to be paid in three installments. True to his nature, as soon as he received the first installment, Chekhov gave 5,000 for the building of a new school in Yalta. Another 1,000 went to his brother Alexander, who had quit drinking and needed money for a new house. He also helped pay for the education of the daughter of a man who had been a mistreated apprentice in Pavel's shop in Taganrog.

Meanwhile, the birth of the Moscow Art Theater in 1898 marked the beginning of an enormous change for Russian drama. The creators of the new theater were the writer-director Nemirovich and the actor-producer Stanislavsky, both about Chekhov's age. Like Chekhov, they wanted to replace the traditional stiff, overblown style of acting with a more natural style. But when they asked Chekhov to let them produce his play *The Seagull*, he hesitated.

The first performance of *The Seagull* in St. Petersburg in October of 1896 had been a disaster. Hastily rehearsed, badly interpreted by the actors, and misunderstood by the audience, it was greeted with jeers, hisses, and catcalls. Chekhov left the theater after the second act and walked the streets until two a.m. The next day he fled from the city swearing never to write for the stage again. There had been other performances, better done, which had received good reviews, but Chekhov still remembered the experience with horror. However, when Nemirovich, who was his friend, assured him that this time there would be careful rehearsals at which he could be present to offer advice, he relented.

On September 9, 1898, in Moscow for a rehearsal of *The Seagull*, Anton Chekhov met Olga Knipper. It was the beginning of the love story that was the last chapter of his life, and like most Chekhovian stories about love it was bittersweet. The thirty-eight year old bachelor had resisted the matchmaking efforts of his friends for many years. As a handsome, famous writer he had many women friends, and many women with the object of matrimony had pursued him. A few of them became his lovers—but probably not as many as claimed after his death to have had an affair with him. Now, as his health was deteriorating and his energy burning low, he met a woman who aroused his interest as no other woman had, and the attraction was mutual.

Olga Knipper was eight years younger than Chekhov. Her parents were German, but her father became a Russian citizen, and she grew up in Moscow where she attended a private school. Her father was an engineer and her mother a gifted musician. As long as Olga's father had lived, Olga and her mother were stifled in their career ambitions. He insisted that his wife not perform professionally, and when Olga wanted to join an amateur dramatic circle he forbade it. When he died, leaving behind only debts, it became necessary for them to work. Her mother became a professor of singing at the Philharmonic School in Moscow and Olga taught music. However, she still longed to go on the stage, and finally with her mother's help she gained admittance to the Philharmonic's drama department. Here, Olga spent three years studying with Nemirovich, rushing through classes so she could earn money for her tuition. She had just graduated from the school and joined the Moscow Art Theater's acting troupe when she met Chekhov.

They had hardly become acquainted when gray, rainy weather forced him to leave Moscow and return to the warmth of Yalta. On the opening night of *The Seagull* at the Moscow Art Theater (December 17, 1898) he anxiously waited for news. The actors, who were also very edgy, had taken valerian drops to sooth their nerves. In their memoirs both Nemirovich and Stanislavsky described the event with a kind of awe. When the curtain fell on the first act. there was silence, complete silence, as though everyone was holding his breath. This mood lasted a long time, so long that the actors looked at each other in horror, and Olga Knipper had difficulty keeping from bursting out sobbing. Then, suddenly, it was as if a dam had burst or a bomb had exploded—all at once there was a deafening crash of applause. The actors were too stunned to bow.

The play ended in triumph with the audience demanding that a telegram of congratulations be sent to the author. Chekhov received the news of the opening night success and of the rave reviews that followed with joy. *The Seagull* continued playing to packed audiences, and congratulatory telegrams and letters poured into Yalta. Chekhov had found a theater where his plays could be successfully interpreted and a place where audiences could understand them. The Moscow Art Theater gratefully acknowledged its debt to Chekhov for its successful launching by adopting a seagull as its permanent emblem. He was encouraged to write more plays. If only he could find the energy to write them.

With the return of spring, Chekhov was again in Moscow. He paid an Easter visit to Olga and her family, and took her to see an exhibition of paintings by his friend Levitan. During the winter Olga and Mariya had become good friends, visiting each other frequently. In May he took Olga with him to Melikhovo to meet Evgenia. Olga was delighted to see the setting where he had written *The Seagull* and created her role of Arkadina. Rain prevented his going to the station to see her off, but immediately they began corresponding, addressing each other as "Dear Actress" and "Dear Writer," and making plans for their next meeting.

In mid-July she came to Yalta where she stayed with family friends. Chekhov was living at a seafront hotel while he supervised the building of his house in Autka. They strolled the seafront together and ate the local fish and drank the local wine in cafés. Olga worried about his health, and tried to get him to eat regular, nourishing meals. In August they traveled together to Moscow; on this visit they became even closer friends. When he had to leave the cold, gray skies of Moscow she sent along a basket filled with good things to sustain him on the trip.

Chekhov and his mother and sister, were now established in their Yalta home. It was light and airy, with an open terrace on the first floor and a glass veranda on the ground floor. The large triple window of his study had a rounded top set with stained glass. From it he could look out on the garden and across the slopes descending to the valley and the town and to the sea beyond. Mountains surrounded the house on three sides, and close to the garden wall was an ancient Tartar cemetery. The fruit trees he had planted and carefully tended were beginning to yield excellent cherries, apricots, peaches, apples, and pears. And his flower garden flourished with an incredible variety of blossoms, including his beloved roses.

Despite the precarious condition of his own health, Chekhov soon became involved in caring for other sick people. Many indigent tubercular patients came to Yalta for the warm climate, and many of them found their way to Dr. Chekhov, who never refused advice or treatment. At times he even took them into his home until he could find lodgings for them. He decided that a hospital was needed in the area and set about raising funds. He wrote appeals that went out all over Russia. Seriously ill people came to Yalta, he told his countrymen, "as though it were a court of final appeal, where the question of life or death will be decided." His appeals raised 40,000 rubles to which he added 5,000 rubles for the building of a sanatorium on the outskirts of Yalta.

Friends and admirers continued to knock on Chekhov's door, often with little regard for his time or privacy. However, he delighted in new friendships with two brilliant young writers who were frequently his chosen companions in his remaining years. Ivan Bunin—painter, poet, and prose writer—was a talented mimic and actor who could make Chekhov laugh. In his memoirs Bunin recalled Chekhov's courage and stoicism in the face of the suffering his illness had caused him in his last years. Chekhov appreciated Bunin's wit and ability and encouraged him in his literary efforts. In 1933 Bunin justified Chekhov's faith in his talent by winning the Nobel Prize for literature.

Maxim Gorky, another young writer who revered Chekhov, initiated their acquaintance by sending him a reverent fan letter and two volumes of his hugely successful *Stories*. They met in Yalta in March of 1899 and bonded in a warm friendship that brought happiness to Chekhov's last years, although their personalities were considerably different. After a harsh childhood, Gorky had wandered about over southern Russia, leading the life of a tramp. He turned his experiences into brilliant short stories that gained him fame in 1898. Chekhov introduced him into literary circles and offered him advice on his writing.

Gorky was hotheaded and often involved in revolutionary causes, while Chekhov hated violence from any source and had always resisted being drawn into politics. Nevertheless, when a wave of student riots swept from St. Petersburg throughout Russia, Chekhov wrote and spoke openly, condemning government brutality against the protesting students who were being thrown into jail and expelled from their universities. The government, he said, had clearly overstepped its rights. When Suvorin wrote articles supporting the government action and Chekhov criticized his stand, it caused a rift in their relationship. However, they continued to correspond and to meet, albeit infrequently. Fortunately, the friendship proved too deep to be destroyed by a difference in ideology.

In April of 1900 the Moscow Art Company went on a road tour to the Crimea. Their repertoire included *The Seagull* and *Uncle Vanya*, an earlier play of Chekhov's which they had revived. Olga came to Yalta a few days ahead of the company, and Chekhov proudly showed her the house and the garden, including two cranes that had taken up residence there. Following their performances in Sevastopol and Yalta the company was strewn with flowers by admirers and royally entertained. Chekhov threw a party for them at Autka to which he invited notable artists and writers such as Gorky, Bunin, and Sergei Rachmaninoff, the composer and pianist. Tea tables were set up on the terrace, in the garden, and in the study. Olga and Mariya served trays of refreshments while Chekhov beamed on his guests. He made the actors feel so at home that they made daily pilgrimages to visit him for lunch or tea. A rich patron invited the company to a farewell luncheon on the roof of her mansion. "At that time," Olga wrote in her memoirs, "we were all hope, liveliness and joy."

Olga spent her holidays during the month of July in Yalta with Chekhov and his family. Almost two years of friendship and flirtation had passed since they met, and during this visit they became lovers. After the family had gone to bed she crept up the creaking stairs to his bedroom in the long white dress he liked. Evgenia and Mariya must have known of the midnight meetings, but had to pretend to be blind and deaf. Perhaps they were not too worried. Chekhov had survived many infatuations and even romances without serious consequences.

From this time their letters appeared more affectionate. They used the familiar form of "you" and more endearing pet names. Chekhov described himself as bored, moping, out of sorts. "I keep thinking the door's going to open and you'll come in," he told her, while she wrote of her fast-paced, exciting life and continually urged him to come to Moscow. Chekhov was hard at work on his new play for the Art Theater and claimed to be chained to his desk in Yalta. The writing went slowly, for which he blamed visitors and bad health. To soothe Olga's impatience he teased her, "Oh, what a part you're going to have in *Three Sisters*! What a part! Give me ten rubles and I'll make sure you get it; otherwise, I'll give it to another actress."

Finally on October 23 Chekhov arrived in Moscow with the manuscript of *Three Sisters*. After settling in at the Dresden Hotel, he began attending rehearsals and performances of various plays at the Art Theater every day and gadding about until late at night with Olga, Gorky, and other friends until he was exhausted. Olga dropped in at his hotel between rehearsals, bringing chocolates, flowers, and other amusing gifts such as a crystal sow followed by three piglets. The samovar would be set up, and she would prepare tea and bread and honey. Heavy velvet curtains shut out the snow and the dark and created an intimate atmosphere for the lovers.

When Stanislavsky arranged for a reading of *Three Sisters* to the Art Theater Company, Chekhov was chagrined by their reaction. They found it unfinished, unactable, and a mystery as to whether it was a comedy or tragedy. He began work on major revisions, but suddenly left Moscow before he finished them. Rumors abounded in Moscow and in St. Petersburg that Chekhov and Olga Knipper were engaged to be married, and she encouraged him: "I have a feeling something beautiful and strong will come of our love," she wrote on the day he departed. But though he wrote of his enduring love for her that would last at least "fifteen years," he remained elusive on the subject of marriage.

He spent the rest of the winter in Nice and in Italy. He revised *Three Sisters*, and after it went into rehearsal he wrote detailed explanations to Olga as to how to play the part of Masha—the character he had created for her. He also had definite ideas about the rest of the production. He was afraid, above all, that the exuberant Stanislavsky would overdo the staging of his subtle drama, and sent specific instructions for how lines and even sound effects should be rendered. Restless as always, Chekhov returned once again to Yalta to write. Olga's letters were filled with the successes of the Art Theater in Moscow and in St. Petersburg, while his were brief and said little about his deteriorating health—although they often mentioned his loneliness and boredom in what he referred to as his "hot Siberia."

In the spring Olga came to Yalta for two weeks. During this visit the awkwardness of their situation became clear. It was embarrassing for everyone to pretend that they were simply good friends. In Russia at that time cohabitation was not an acceptable way of life for people of their class. Apparently an understanding was reached, and a few days after she left he wrote to her: "If you give me your word that not a soul in Moscow will hear anything about our marriage until the moment it takes place, I will marry you, if you like, on the very day I arrive." He added that all was well at home except for one "small detail"—his health.

When Chekhov arrived in Moscow in mid-May, he was examined by doctors who advised him to go as soon as possible to a government sanatorium in the Ufa district to take the koumiss (mare's milk) cure. This treatment was popular at that time, and Chekhov agreed to try it. The sanatorium would have to be their honeymoon destination.

Despite the well-known fact that Chekhov had a horror of any kind of ceremony where he was the central figure, he does seem to have behaved rather callously toward his family in regard to his marriage. The wedding took place on May 25, 1901, in the Church of the Exaltation of the Cross in Moscow. The four witnesses required by law were present: Olga's brother and an uncle and two students. Friends and relatives in Moscow were invited to a dinner well away from the church, where they finally realized that the bride and groom were not going to appear. Back in Yalta, Evgenia and Mariya received a telegram informing them that the ceremony had taken place. The faithful Mariya was particularly shattered by the news.

The newlyweds enjoyed the scenery in the remote area of their honeymoon, but eventually grew tired of mare's milk and rough living accommodations. On July 1, in less than the two months scheduled stay, they were sailing back down the Volga on their way to Yalta.

When rehearsals began at the Art Theater in August, Olga had to return to Moscow. Six years earlier when Suvorin had urged him to marry, Chekhov had lightheartedly replied he would consider it if he could have a wife "...who, like the moon, would not appear day after day on my horizon." An unkind fate granted his wish. During the three years of their marriage the amount of time they were apart and the amount of time they were together were almost equal.

When they were separated they wrote each other daily. Olga repeatedly expressed her longing to be with him, but she also described her stage successes, all-night parties, delicious dinners, dancing in nightclubs in a golden dress. In letter after letter she reproached herself for not giving up the stage to be with him in Yalta. When she expressed remorse for deserting him, he repeatedly assured her he was happy she had a successful career. In a letter dated December 29, 1901, he told her: "You're a goose, sweetheart. Never, while I'm your husband, will I take you away from the theatre; on the contrary, I'm delighted that you have something to do, that you have a goal in life...." But he also wrote, "It's deadly dull without you. I'm used to you, like a child, and without you I have no comfort or warmth."

Both of them longed to have a child, and Olga became pregnant but suffered a miscarriage at the end of March 1902. She went to Yalta to recuperate, but she felt, probably with reason, that Evgenia and Mariya blamed her love of partying and nightlife for causing the mishap. Chekhov returned with her to Moscow where he nursed her devotedly through a serious bout of peritonitis—despite the fact that he, himself, was weak and coughing blood.

Back in Yalta, although he found his creative energy waning and writing increasingly wearying, Chekhov managed to produce three major works. The short story published in 1902, "The Bishop," about a dying clergyman, seems a summary of his own life as a dying author. The last short story he wrote was "The Bride" (sometimes called "The Betrothed" or "The Fiancée" in English), a remarkable story about a young woman who frees herself from the traditional roles that her family and society try to force on her. Leaving her fiancée and the nice home he has prepared for her, she escapes to St. Petersburg to study. At the end of the story she is eagerly looking forward to life as an independent woman. An appealing character in the story is Sasha, a young revolutionary, who is dying of tuberculosis.

Work on *The Cherry Orchard*, the play he had promised for the Art Theater's season opener, was painfully slow. He squeezed it out line by line, returning to his bed after writing half a page. Nemirovich and Stanislavsky and Olga pushed him to finish it, but he would not send it to them until he had polished it to suit his exacting standards. When he finally sent it, the producers received it with such enthusiasm that his suspicions were aroused. He was afraid they would overdo and turn into heavy drama what he insisted was a comedy.

He was eager to follow the manuscript to Moscow, but his Yalta doctor was opposed to his going there in winter. As a physician Chekhov must have known he was right. The slightest exertion made him short of breath; his ears buzzed; he had fierce headaches; coughing fits interrupted his attempts to write; and intestinal upsets constantly plagued him. Nevertheless on December 2, defying his doctor's orders, he fled to Moscow. The dry, cold air and Olga's company at first seemed to put new life into him.

Just as Chekhov had feared, Stanislavsky had ideas about the production of *The Cherry Orchard* that did not agree with his own, but he had appeared on the scene too late to do much about it. The premiere was set for January 17, 1904, to honor Chekhov's forty-fourth birthday and twenty-five years of literary endeavor. Suspecting that he would have to accept honors and congratulatory speeches, Chekhov stayed away on opening night. However, when Nemirovich and Stanislavsky sent for him, saying the actors and audience were demanding his presence, he allowed himself to be dragged onto the stage. For an hour, he endured the outpouring of gifts and speeches, toasts and ovations as best he could. Although the event completely exhausted him, the out-pouring of admiration and affection touched him.

Once back in Yalta, he was too weak to write, although his head and his notebooks were full of ideas. In mid-April he again escaped to Moscow where Olga put him to bed and called in her family doctor, Julius Taube. Dr. Taube gave him morphine injections and placed him on a strict diet. He also wanted him to consult with a Berlin specialist and to go to Badenweiler—a clinic for chest diseases located in the Black Forest of Germany—as soon as he was strong enough to travel. It was June 3 before he was well enough to make the journey.

In Berlin they stayed at the Savoy Hotel, and he wrote Mariya an optimistic letter on June 6 telling her he felt much better and was enjoying seeing the city with Olga. He spoke to her of plans to visit Italy and return to Yalta in August. Dr. Karl Ewald, the specialist recommended by Dr. Taube, examined Chekhov carefully. Then he stood up, shrugged his shoulders, and left without a word of advice or encouragement.

In Badenweiler they found a more sympathetic doctor who treated Chekhov with gentleness and affection. They settled into a sunny room in the Hotel Sommer where they could have lunch and dinner at their own table in the dining room. Chekhov spent hours sitting in the garden or on their balcony, watching with interest the people in the small town as they went in and out of the post office.

The weather turned hot and Chekhov's shortness of breath increased. The last letter he wrote was to Mariya on June 28. He asked her help in finding out about boat schedules as he was thinking of taking a boat trip from Trieste to Odessa. He told her about the new lightweight suit he had ordered. And he mentioned his health almost casually. "The food here is tasty," he told her, "but it does not do me much good. My stomach keeps getting upset. About the only remedy for it is to fast, in other words, to refrain entirely from eating, and that's that. And the only medicine for being short-winded is to keep perfectly still." Typically, he ended the letter with a joke: "There's not a single well-dressed German woman; their lack of taste is depressing."

At dusk on July 1, Olga went to the chemists for oxygen. When she returned, Chekhov seemed stronger. To cheer her up he began making up a funny story about an expensive health spa where rich, overweight guests who were greedily looking forward to a gargantuan meal discovered that the chef had run off. Describing the pampered guests' reaction to this disaster, Chekhov made his wife laugh heartily. Then he lay down to sleep.

At about one o'clock he woke up in great pain and, for the first time in his life, asked that a doctor be sent for. When his doctor came, Chekhov told him *"Ich sterbe"* ("I am dying"). The doctor gave him an injection of camphor and ordered champagne. Taking a full glass, Chekhov smiled at Olga and said, "It's a long time since I drank champagne." He drained the glass and quietly lay down. In a few minutes he stopped breathing, dying as simply and courageously as he had lived.

AFTERWORD

After Chekhov was buried next to his father in the Moscow cemetery, Olga returned with the family to the Yalta home, where she stayed for six weeks. She then went to Moscow to resume play rehearsals. She never married again and maintained a close friendship with Mariya. Even when Stalin made the Moscow Art Theater his official theater, Olga adapted and remained its star performer. After a long, brilliant career, she died in her nineties.

In 1901 Chekhov had made an informal will leaving everything to Mariya. When it was declared invalid, Olga generously renounced all claim to the estate and gave Mariya the money in her and Chekhov's joint account. Chekhov's brothers also renounced any share in the inheritance that might legally have been declared theirs. The faithful Mariya became a rich woman, since she owned the income from Chekhov's plays as well as the house and bank account.

As she had so often done in his lifetime, Mariya set aside her private life to take care of her brother's affairs. She assembled the large collection of memoirs and letters that were published soon after his death. And she kept his heritage intact through the Revolution, through Stalin's destructive reign, and through the German occupation in World War II. When the Yalta house became a museum, she served as its director until she died at the age of ninety-four in 1957. Mariya also took care of their mother, as Chekhov had anticipated she would. Evgenia enjoyed the house and garden and riding in automobiles until she died fifteen years after her famous son had.

In 1929, Boris Poplavsky, a brilliant Russian poet, wrote in his personal journal, "Chekhov can help us live." Chekhov himself said many times, "Man will become better only when you make him see what he is like." In the twenty-first century his wisdom can still help us—if we have ears to hear.

In *Uncle Vanya* a character says, "Man was granted reason and creative abilities to increase that which was given him, but until now he has not created, but destroyed. There are fewer and fewer forests, the rivers dry up, wild animals are dying out, the climate is ruined and with each passing day the earth is becoming poorer and uglier." And another characters exits the stage saying, "You must all do something useful."

Chekhov's own life is a supreme example of a useful life: as a builder of schools, hospitals, and libraries; as a compassionate doctor, family man, and friend; and above all as a writer who told us the truth about the way we are.

MEI CHIN

Exploring the Works of Anton Chekhov

Anton Pavlovich Chekhov, short story writer and dramatist, was a great writer who had missed, by his birth, the great Russian age of writers by a few years and missed, by his death, the Russian Revolution by one. This was the man who palled around with Leo Tolstoy and Maxim Gorky, and quarreled with Konstantin Stanislavsky. This was also the man who, in his writing, breathed new life into the inconclusive. In Chekhov, people drink, they philosophize, they make love, they go insane, they duel. Sometimes they even die, but death, just like sex and fighting, is not a solution. Class conflict is a recurring topic, but not one that is ever worked out. He is an elusive and often frustrating read.

He was just as baffling a person. It is frequently tempting to decipher the character of an author through his work, but if one does this to Chekhov, one should proceed with care. Certainly, Chekhov had no compunction over putting his friends in his works. The unabashedly hilarious story "The Grasshopper," for instance, is an almost blow-by-blow account of the affair between the painter Isaak Levitan and his married mistress Sophia Kusyshinikova. Myriad women, most famously Lydia Avilov and Lika Misinov, have laid claim to his heroines. But whether Chekhov ever wrote himself in his works is debatable. Certainly, he rarely identifies with his heroes. In fact, nothing seems to entrance him more than to write from the point of view of exactly the kind of person whom he holds in contempt.

Contradictions between Chekhov the man and Chekhov the writer abound. The objects of desire in Chekhov are of the slender, sylvan,

61

barely developed sort; yet in reality he preferred robust, not necessarily chaste women with tempers and loud laughs. He writes frequently and feelingly about sex, yet in his own life, we know that he could barely be bothered. Many of his characters feast and drink to voluptuous excess; Chekhov was a moderate man.

However, we do know from his work that he was a man of a mordant humor; his best works ring with it. This is the man who famously argued with the director Stanislavsky; Chekhov insisting that the plays be staged as farces, Stanislavsky insisting on jerking from his audience the largest volumes of tears. No one can forget poor Osip Dymov, cuckolded husband of "The Grasshopper's" Olga Ivanova, "rubbing his hands together, and saying, 'Come to supper gentlemen!'" to his wife's crowd of parasitic artists. Slapstick abounds, especially in the form of misfired bullets—Uncle Vanya taking potshots at Serebryakov; the macho Von Korem taking careful aim at his milk-toast nemesis Layevsky and then being distracted at the last minute by the hysterics of the local deacon. Then there is the priceless squabble between Chebutykin and Solynony in the *Three Sisters* about whether a certain dish is made out of meat or onion.

There is another thing about which we can be certain. Chekhov changed his mind almost as often as his characters. "… (H)is motives and opinions," writes Ronald Hingley, "were apt to change radically from one moment to another." But, in Hingley's words, "That human personality is ultimately an enigma" (Hingley, 1) was the only thing about which Chekhov was sure.

Anton Pavlovich Chekhov was born on January 17, 1860, in the southern Russian town of Taganrog, which, at thirty thousand inhabitants was almost a city. There were local Greek millionaires, a library, and even an opera house, but there was also the typical industrial soot and the ramshackle one-story houses. As with many other things in his life, Chekhov's attitude towards his hometown was mixed. He called it "dirty, drab, empty, lazy, and illiterate." It was, for him, the essence of a Russian provincial town, which he held in great contempt. "I don't like Taganrog manners, can't bear them, I would think, would run to the ends of the earth to avoid them." (Callow, 6). And yet he returned from time to time; he also donated money to its library. The town figures, albeit not very poetically, in several of his stories, and on one occasion he rhapsodized that it was "Asia, pure and simple!"

His father, Pavel Chekhov, was a grocer and former serf. Young Anton Chekhov grew up helping out his father in a grocery that smelled of tallow, herrings, and vodka, and that was open from five in the morning until midnight. It was the life of a poorer tradesman, which accounts for the vividness with which Chekhov would portray these people later on. Accounts of Pavel Chekhov vary. His children Mariya and Mikhail laud him as a talented, passionate man who played the fiddle, discussed politics, and dressed immaculately even when he was on the verge of bankruptcy. But Mariya and Mikhail's accounts are published almost specifically as a counter to the riotous account published by their oldest brother Alexander, which depicts a religious fanatic who beat his sons and his clerks on impulse, cheated his customers, and bullied his wife. Alexander's most vivid anecdote was of finding a rat drowned in a vat of cooking oil. Pavel called in the local priest to bless the oil, then sold it anyway. Chekhov seems to be in accordance with Alexander. "We felt," he once wrote, "like little convicts." (Callow, 8). Perhaps Chekhov's most autobiographical passages relate to his father. The protagonist Laptev's father of "Three Years" is also a merchant, albeit a wealthier one than Pavel, but he is also a religious fanatic, terrifies his staff, and makes his children work in a warehouse at a young age. Laptev says:

> ... my mother had been worn out by terror. I can remember my father correcting me—or, to speak plainly, beating me—before I was five years old. He used to thrash me with a birch, pull my ears, hit me on the head ... I'm afraid of religion, and when I pass a church I remember my childhood and am overcome by horror.

In a passage reminiscent of the anecdote about the rat, the narrator of "My Life" recalls, "My father took bribes and imagined that they were given him out of respect for his moral qualities."

Despite his shopkeeper status, Pavel Chekhov was not a man of the people. While asserting that Pavel was a temperamental man, V. S. Pritchett also points to Pavel's Mr. Micawber leanings (Pritchett, 12). After all, he was a man who was proud of his moral fiber, his violin, his education, his collection of old newspapers, and who strolled down the avenue with his daughter and wife in a starched shirt front, frock coat, and top hat. Nor were his offspring typical populist fodder. All of the Chekhov children boasted a university education. Even Mariya, the one girl of the family, received a diploma from Rajevski University and became a schoolteacher.

In many ways, Chekhov was representative of his turbulent times, which was why he became a favorite of the revolutionaries. (The Russian Revolution occurred a year after his death.) In Chekhov's day, the serfs had been freed, poverty and disease ran amok among the peasantry, and yet the upper classes were running out of money and were useless. Money was to be made by sons of serfs, merchants who had gone to university but were still deeply conscious of their roots. Chekhov was, after all, a member of the latter category. By remaking himself as a doctor and a writer, he almost seems a symbol of the potential of the common man. But one wonders what might have been his response to such radical adoration. For one thing, he has none of the lyrical views shared by the well-bred Tolstoy and Turgenev. One might say that his class consciousness was cynical because he had been through it all. His experiences were the disillusioned ones of an upstart. Rampant through his stories are men who try to better themselves—landowners who aid their tenants, daughters of factory workers who grow up to be factory owners, shopkeepers' sons who aspire to marry rich girls. In the end, such efforts are for naught. The peasants will always hate their landlords, no matter how much the landlords try to help them. Anna Akimovna of "A Woman's Kingdom" sits in her rich house longing to return to the humble life of a worker's daughter. Even the compassionate merchant Lopakhin of *The Cherry Orchard* never overcomes his pedigree as an embittered son of serfs. He gloats, "Come here, all of you, and you just watch Yermolay Lopakhin get his axe into that cherry orchard, watch the trees come crashing down ... Music, boys!"

We have to take time to discuss the members of the Chekhov family, all of whom figure importantly in his writing. There was his illiterate, gentle mother, whom he loved and, whose humiliations by his bullying father made him shrink in pain, often appears as the haggard woman in stories like "Three Years," "My Life," and "Difficult People." Though completely unlike Gertrude, she is the engenderer of countless Chekhovian Hamlets. His persistently amorous younger brother Mikhail made an appearance in "About Love." The formidable sister Mariya nursed and loved him steadfastly throughout his life; he loved her back and yet was suffocated by her; after his death, it was she who was responsible for censoring much of his correspondence.

It was Chekhov's older brothers, Alexander and Nikolai, who initially showed the most artistic promise in the family. Alexander was a talented writer and Nikolai a talented painter, and they both escaped as soon as possible to university in Moscow. Both encouraged him aesthetically; the young Anton Chekhov looked up to the oldest brother Alexander especially. For instance, when Anton confessed a liking for Harriet Beecher Stowe, Alexander urged him to consider Maupassant instead.

Nothing is worse for a boy than to be left behind by the people that he loves. Such was young Chekhov's plight when Pavel became bankrupt and fled with the family to Moscow. Abandonment runs rampant through Chekhov's work. The story that is arguably the most personal, not in fact, but in mood, is "The Steppe." This almost novella chronicles the journey of Yegorushka, who, after being entrusted to the care of his uncle and a priest, finds himself abandoned to journey along the stretching steppe terrain with a group of peasants. The similarities between Chekhov's story and his life are many: Yegorushka is nine years old, Chekhov is fifteen; and while Yegorushka is traveling, Chekhov is left behind. Still, they must have both "felt the most abject of mortals and wanted to cry." "Had they forgotten him?" Chekhov writes. "At the thought that he had been forgotten and left to the mercy of fate he felt chilled and so frightened."

It is also interesting to note that Yegorushka is traveling so that he can go to school, while Chekhov is living on his own so that he could stay in it. "The Steppe" was one of the works that marked the turning point of Chekhov's career. It is a careening, almost surreal work through the rural Russian landscape. The young hero begins with his uncle and a philosophizing priest and ends up in the company of traveling peasants. The story had been inspired by his grandmother's adventures as she traveled through the Russian steppes to visit her husband's grave. Landscape, in "The Steppe," is as vivid as cut glass.

> The air became even more immobile from the heat and the silence, and submissive nature was numbed from that deathly hush. No wind, not one bright fresh sound, not even one small cloud.

Though "The Steppe" is a coming-of-age story, it is not a conventional one. Boy goes on journey, forms relationships, is abandoned, forms more relationships, and then discovers that he will be alone for the rest of his life. Yet it does not follow the ordinary narrative arc. "The Steppe" is told in terms of feeling, specifically that of a young boy. Nature is seen through the eyes of someone who is frightened and very, very small. Hence, seemingly slight moments take on monumental proportions for the boy. What remains in this child's mind of this journey are the "dragonflies and feathers" that "soared towards the heavens in a black rotating column and darkened the sun." There is the woman who bends to kiss him when she thinks that he is asleep— "velvety black eyebrows, dimpled female cheeks, from which her smile radiated like sunbeams." There is the strange, lackluster figure of Vasya, who spots a vixen in a distance, "playing like a little dog." There is the stew of crayfish and fish that smells of "fishy wetness" and is cluttered with scales. Above all, there is the idle, handsome, cruel Dymov, one of the companions on Yegorushka's journey, the type of man every sensitive boy hates. "Hit him," Yegorushka screams with tears in his eyes, "Hit him!" His loneliness at the end of the story is far from existential.

> … with these two men, all that he had lived through until then had vanished forever, like smoke. He sank exhausted, shedding bitter tears as he greeted that new, unknown life that was just beginning for him.

Yegorushka may always be alone, but he will always long for another's company. Safe to say, Chekhov feels more deeply for this young Yegorushka than he does for many of his later characters. We can say, perhaps, that because "The Steppe" is one of his most melancholy stories, it is also one of his most intimately felt.

At the age of nineteen, Anton Chekhov rejoined his family in Moscow, where the reunion was considerably less lyrical than he had imagined. He found them residing in two-room dilapidated quarters, with his drunk father and an equally intoxicated Alexander living in a different apartment with a common-law wife, his fierce creativity already in rapid deterioration. Nikolai, too, was following in his older brother's boozy, lecherous footsteps. This would be the beginning of Chekhov's most potent heartbreak. Nikolai would develop an addiction to morphine before he eventually succumbed to tuberculosis. Alexander would be the greatest disappointment, with a string of mistreated mistresses, an ever-expanding household, and his constant demands for money. In the end, Chekhov's ambivalence towards his former heroes cemented his trademark attitude of detachment, in his literature as well as in his life. As a man, he loved but left ample room to hold back. As a writer, he never loved his characters too much.

It was in Moscow that he began studying to be a doctor, as well as contributing short pieces to the weekly comic Moscow magazines at the urging of Alexander. Chekhov wrote under the pen name of Antosha Chekhonte and turned out sixty pieces in two years. Later, he would write for the editor Nikolai Leykin, at *Splinters* magazine, before being won over by the right-wing millionaire and plutocrat Aleksey Suvorin, on whose payroll Chekhov would discover the seeds of true literary freedom. Ultimately Suvorin would allow enough room in his newspaper *The New Times* for the one hundred plus pages of young Chekhov's seminal piece "The Steppe." In 1886, he received correspondence from Dmitri Gregorovich, former flatmate of Dostoevsky and at the time considered one of Russian literature's true grandpapas. "You have real talent," Gregorovich wrote. Chekhov was overwhelmed. "I can only repeat that I was thunderstruck," he replied (Karlinsky, 58). Gregorovich urged Chekhov to begin writing not for deadlines (Chekhov easily turned out a story a day) but for perfection, and also to publish under his real name.

Often, Chekhov's early work is dismissed as the first tentative efforts of a man who would become a master. But plenty of early Chekhov is deeply affecting; when read today, many of these stories seem more modern than his later work. Quite a few are breathlessly brief; snapshots rather than stories, glimpses into lives that, as in real life, have no proper conclusion. He gives us almost painstakingly detailed entry into a handful of hours. While later Chekhov characters are effusive, and sometimes unreal in their eloquence, the characters in his early stories are reserved. When they do talk, their speech is elliptical; they rarely say what they feel and they never philosophize. In "Anyuta," the title character stands half-naked in the middle of a grimy apartment while her medical student lover draws her ribs with a crayon. She says only seven words in the entire story, among them "Your hands are cold!" When the student asks her to pack her things and leave, the whole of her devastation is crystallized in simple gestures and a stammered phrase.

> Anyuta put on her coat again, in silence wrapped up her embroidery in paper, gathered together her needles and thread; she found the screw of paper with the four lumps of sugar in the window and laid it on the table by the books.
> "That's … your … sugar …" she said softly.

In "Agafya," the heroine has an adulterous affair with an indolent, woman-hating, handsome young peasant. Again, she says little. The most powerful image is of her "exhaling noisily" after a gulp of vodka. When the train bearing Agafya's husband returns, Agafya ignores it. In the morning, she is left to her husband's mercy.

> Never before have I seen anyone, drunk or sober, walking like that. Agafya seemed to be thrown into convulsions by her husband's looks. She was zigzagging across the field, stopping dead, marking time, her legs giving way under her, and her arms floundering about helplessly, or walking backwards.

In "The Huntsman," a woman and a hunter share a few words on the road on a day when "everything living was hiding from the heat." It becomes apparent that the woman is the man's wife, and that he has hardly seen her in the twelve years that they have been married, except on the odd occasion that he comes home drunk and beats her. Still, there is "sadness and tender affection … Her gaze flitted over her husband's tall, lean figure and caressed and fondled it." The story ends with her standing "on tiptoe to see the white cap (of the huntsman) once more."

Each of these stories—all of them under ten pages in length—is marked with a poignant evocation of atmosphere. The dirty cigarette butts swimming in the pail of the student's room. The "sun-baked grass … disconsolate, hopeless" in "The Huntsman." The idyllic landscape in "Agafya," with its willow trees astir. Already, Chekhov is demonstrating an admirable insight into the female psyche. These women speak little, and yet somehow in their movements he is able to convey "reckless determination, weakness, and pain." Yet the narrative remains detached.

We expect to feel sorry for these women, and yet, by restricting the descriptions to surface detail only, Chekhov forces us to restrain our judgment. We are merely confused, and vaguely depressed.

"Misery" is the last of these early stories discussed in this essay. Together with "Agafya," it is one of the first stories to which he penned his real name. The story is almost puritan. A cabdriver has just lost his son, and cannot find anyone to talk about it. He finally finds solace murmuring the night away to his mare. It is a fantastic example of the expert handling that Chekhov applies to potentially sodden material. There is no grandness about the grieving in "Misery." The emotional core of the story is contained in visceral flashes—the cab customers in the night, the yawning colleagues in the cab yard, and the fleeting thoughts of Iona, the cabdriver. Grief is juxtaposed with everyday hurly-burly activities. Life is cruel because it continues on its pragmatic way:

> And Iona turns round to tell them how his son died, but at
> that point the hunchback gives a faint sigh and announces
> that, thank God! They have arrived at last.

The protagonist is not a cabdriver-cum-poet; he is an ordinary old man. Mourning for his son is juxtaposed with the "big flakes of wet snow" whirling, the sight of his little white mare, delicate as a gingerbread horse, and financial worries. "[Iona] thinks about oats, about hay, about the weather." Ultimately, it makes his grief more poignant.

> If Iona's heart were to burst and his misery were to flow out,
> it would flood the whole world, it seems, and yet it is not
> seen. It has found a hiding place in such an insignificant shell
> that one would not have found it with a candle by daylight.

Grief is rawer when it is ordinary. The beauty of Chekhov's early work is its simplicity, a quality which some of his later, more celebrated works lack.

Though Chekhov had cemented his reputation as a writer by the 1880's, he still considered himself, first and foremost, a doctor. Medicine, he frequently said, was his wife, and writing was his mistress. Medicine also had a tremendous impact upon his writing, for Chekhov would always be a tremendously clinical writer. As a doctor, he saw that

death is not overblown in the Tolstoyan manner, but that it is often weak
and an anti-climax, while in the background, life goes on its murmuring
way. We see this in the almost flippant suicides in *Ivanov* and *The Seagull*;
the swift deathbed scenes in stories like "The Grasshopper"; the
homicide in "Murder." There is something forensic, yet witty, about
murderers stepping gingerly around a piece of potato steeped in their
victim's blood. The body of the title character in "Gusev" is thrown
overboard in a shoddy ceremony; and then his death is immediately
eclipsed by the magnificence of the sea, and the green, lilac, and purple
lights in the sky:

> ... the ocean frowns at first, but before long it too takes on
> gentle, ardent hues which are difficult to name in the
> language of man.

Chekhov had treated his brother Alexander's first common-law
wife as she lay dying of tuberculosis. More traumatically, he treated his
brother Nikolai as he lay dying of the same disease. Chekhov channeled
Nikolai's death into "A Dreary Story," a tale where death is matter of
fact. The hero, also named Nikolai, prepares to face his impending end
with a shrug. The result is one of Chekhov's most devastating works.
Chekhov himself had begun spitting blood, and it is interesting to note
that Chekhov made his hero a doctor-scientist, a profession closer to his
own than to that of his painter brother. Perhaps we can venture to say
that "A Dreary Story" is both an ode to his brother and a document of
Chekhov's own struggle with mortality.

The icy eye of science is Nikolai's only comfort. He says:

> Now that I am on the brink of death only science has any
> interest for me ... When I draw my last breath I shall still
> believe that science is the most important, beautiful, and vital
> thing in man's life.

Personal echoes abound. The university where Nikolai teaches is a
duplicate of the university at which Chekhov studied: "grim gates ...
which have not been repaired for ages, a bored caretaker in sheepskin, a
broom, heaps of snow ..." And most tellingly, "Such gates can hardly
produce a wholesome impression on a lad fresh from the provinces who

imagines that the temple of science is really a temple." For the eager young Chekhov was crestfallen upon arriving at this highly lauded institution.

But tuberculosis remains the story's most powerful presence. In those days, it was the Russian disease; Tolstoy's first wife died of it. It was thought to be a genetic condition, and Chekhov had many relatives with tuberculosis on his mother's side, as did Nikolai in the story. Nevertheless, Chekhov denied his own symptoms. The blood in his lungs, he claimed, was due to a broken blood vessel; it was a myth that he continued to perpetuate until the very end of his life. V. S. Pritchett writes that consumptives "tend to conceal their fears by doubling the fervor of their imagination and especially their feverish yet detached appetite for living, seeing, feeling and their denial for what is within them." (Callow, 63). Certainly this explains the feverish creativity of consumptive artists. But it is particularly potent in the case of Chekhov, given that he was a medical man. In denying his condition, he was struggling against the scientific facts in which he had been trained.

Denial fascinated him, and he examined it with surgical precision. Throughout his work, he dissected the ways in which people delude themselves in the face of death and in love; also the ways in which denial paralyzes those whom it possesses. Helena and Astrov deny their passion for each other in *Uncle Vanya*; Gusev denies the fact that he will never live to see his hometown. In many ways, Nikolai of "A Dreary Story" is also in denial. While he accepts his death sentence intellectually, he refuses treatment and is determined to continue working. In fact, it takes Nikolai a long time to tell the reader about his condition. "As regards to my present life, I must first mention the insomnia from which I have begun to suffer lately." He takes us through a list of the other things in his life, which are organized, it would seem, in order of importance—insomnia at the top, then the monotony of his relationship with his wife, the coldness of his daughter, and his lectures. His impending death is mentioned like an aforethought, for in Nikolai's dull world, death is the dullest.

Above all, Nikolai refuses compassion in his effort to shut his eyes to death, particularly from the only person left in his life that he loves—the girl Katya. Katya urges him to take her money, for in many ways their relationship is the only thing that sustains her as well. "You could go away for treatment somewhere. You must get good medical treatment," she says. "Will you take it? Will you? Darling, will you?" He refuses. And in the story's tormented conclusion, Katya is on her knees, crying, imploring for "Just one word. Only one word. What shall I do?" Nikolai denies her, and rather awkwardly tells her to stop crying and have breakfast. At that last denial, Katya transforms.

> Her hand is cold, like the hand of a stranger … She goes out of my room and walks along the long passage without looking back … I catch a glimpse of her black dress for the last time, the sound of her footsteps dies away … Good-bye my treasure.

Doctors abound in Chekhov. Besides Nikolai there is Astrov from *Cherry Orchard*, Lvov from *Ivanov*, Samoylenko from "The Duel," Ragin in "Ward Six," just to name a few. The Chekhov doctor is a self-made man, educated but not elite. By virtue of his profession, however, he is able to penetrate the milieu of aristocrats, and often respects them as his superiors. As he writes about Samoylenko in "The Duel,"

> The fact that Layevsky was once a university student … and often spoke so cleverly that only few could understand him, that he was living with a woman of culture—all this was beyond Samoylenko's understanding and it pleased him.

The doctor also consorts with the poor, and this mobility gives him the capacity of observer. He is fascinated by physical and psychological weakness; in the case of Ragin in "Ward Six," such a fascination proves fatal. When he is combined with high moral principles like Lvov, he is insufferable. When blessed with brilliance and angst, he becomes as hopeless as Astrov.

Perhaps no doctor is closer to Chekhov's heart than Samoylenko from "The Duel." Cheerful and seemingly idiotic in his boundless good temper, Samoylenko is the man whom no one can hate. On closer observation, however, it becomes apparent that Samoylenko is no fool. He is the one character who refuses to pass judgment, or for that matter, become restricted to one point of view. His stupidity is in fact superb subtlety. The fiery zoologist Von Koren grumbles, "You're equally indifferent to everyone." It is a comment that arguably could be applied to Chekhov himself.

While Samoylenko is one of Chekhov's more likeable doctors, Lvov makes us flinch. Chekhov writes that he is an "honest, straightforward, hot-headed, but narrow-minded and limited man ... a stereotype personified." (Heim, 79) Indeed, Ronald Hingley argues that in writing the character of Lvov, Chekhov was castigating himself. It was 1887. Chekhov was overworking as both a doctor and writer to support his parents and siblings. (Chekhov, who did not marry until late, would ultimately provide for his family for the rest of his life.) Alexander and Nikolai—who was still alive at the time, but very ill—were hopeless debauches, and Chekhov condemned them both. (Hingley, 92) Perhaps Lvov is less "narrow-minded" than Chekhov claims. After all, he has a perfectly clear-headed picture of the other characters' motives, especially those of Ivanov. What makes him limited is his disapproval. It was as if Chekhov, through Lvov, was portraying a side of himself that he would successfully annihilate in his writing, but never quite overcome in his personal life.

Ivanov is Chekhov's first full-length play, after completing the minor work *Platonov* at the age of twenty. Ivanov was finished in a breathless ten days, Chekhov's response to a request for a light-hearted comedy. Naturally, any comedy that involves the death of a sweet woman from tuberculosis, and the so-called hero dying suddenly at the end (in the first version, Ivanov expires from a heart attack; in the second, with the help of a pistol) is no ordinary comedy. Moreover, it challenges the audience's moral assumptions. We are made to like Ivanov, a lazy landowner who, while his loving wife Anna lies dying, makes eyes at the virginal twenty-year-old next door. We dislike Lvov, who, with all his preaching, is fundamentally a good man, half in love with Anna, whose sole purpose in life is to make sure that people treat each other properly. Most of the supporting characters are fundamentally debauched; they either sponge off rich families, engage in domestic squabbles, or scheme to marry the rich widow Martha Babakin.

Yet *Ivanov* is hilarious. "Uncle," complains Ivanov, "you're always popping up, one can never talk in peace." And indeed, people are always "popping up"; windows open, faces appear, doors slam. Dialogue is at a relentless pace. The ideal way to stage *Ivanov* is as a screwball comedy, with the minor characters as clowns. The wizened, penniless uncle Shabelesky, always on the brink of melodramatic tears; the mercenary

Borkin, whom I see as fat and pink in the face; the countless parasitic guests at the Lebedevs playing cards with Avodoya, who is beautifully described as "an old woman with no definite means of support." There is also the widow Babakin, "the one like a washerwoman," in the words of one character, whom one sees in overly flamboyant dresses and jewels as she sweeps in armed with pouting comments such as "I can't pretend to be all that young." (To which one of the guests replies gallantly, "You put all the young girls in the shade.") Many critics call *Ivanov* conventional, a transitional work. I find it quite winning. But the most fundamental thing about *Ivanov* is that it cannot be played glum. For the comedy in *Ivanov* is purely physical; if you put Babakin and Avodya and Borkin in drab clothes and serious demeanors, the light of the play is gone. This would be central in Chekhov's theatre, something that would resound also in his more satiric short stories. Heartbreak and the ridiculous share the same bed. Tears, especially the ones wept by other people, are mawkish. Nothing better sums this up in *Ivanov* than this early exchange:

> *Shabelesky*: I'd sit by my wife's grave and think for days on end. I'd just sit there until I died. She's buried in Paris. (Pause)
> *Anna*: It's terribly boring. Shall we play another duet?

Of all people, the dying Anna should be touched by this tribute to dead wives. She is not.

Opening night was on November 19, 1887. None of the actors knew their lines, and one was "as drunk as a lord." (Karlinsky, 72). Perhaps Chekhov, though horrified, could appreciate the sublime irony. The play was a farce, but not in the way that the author had intended. But *Ivanov* was not a failure, despite the fact that Chekhov wrote to Suvorin, "it's too early for me to undertake playwriting." (Karlinsky, 82).

The next summer, desperate to escape his Moscow success, he took a cottage on an estate called Luka. Summering in the country was not new to Chekhov; he had taken a cottage at Babinko for the past three summers running, a cottage that would make numerous appearances in his writing, most notably in *The Cherry Orchard*. It was at Luka, however, that he would meet the extraordinary Lintarev family. In his lifetime, Chekhov cultivated relationships with many famous people, among them Leo Tolstoy, Maxim Gorky, Konstantin Stanislavsky, Alexei

Suvorin, and the landscape painter Isaak Levitan. Stanislavsky established himself as *the* director of Chekhov's important plays; young Gorky idolized him, whereas the aging Tolstoy always found something nice to say about his work, even though most of the later pieces are deliberately anti-Tolstoyian.

But it is the quieter intercourse with the Lintarev family that I will focus upon, because in many ways it was just as influential, and perhaps even more poignant. The Lintarevs lived in an old manor house; they were educated and eloquent and deeply attractive; they were moderately liberal; they played instruments and read books. All five of the children were unmarried. The mother read Schopenhauer. One son was untalented but honest, recently expelled from university; the other played the piano. But it was the Lintarev daughters who exerted the most fascination. The youngest daughter was one of those ruddy intellectual types who dreamed of bourgeois marriage but had read Karl Marx and was "too homely" to make a good match.

The two older daughters were both doctors. The oldest was blind from a brain tumor that would eventually kill her. She, reports Chekhov, "speaks stoically and with remarkable sang-froid about her approaching death." She chuckled and she joked, the peasants referred to her as a saint, and Chekhov, who had been exposed to plenty of people on the verge of death, finally realized that "instead of feeling the approach of our own deaths we write ... as though we were never going to die." It was a theme that he would approach less than a year later in "A Dreary Story." In her merry attitude was exemplified the Chekhovian notion of tragedy and laughter co-existing. Moreover, Chekhov at this moment was experiencing attacks of coughing and blood spitting, with increased frequency and violence. With his own days numbered, the eldest Lintarev daughter might have provided some subconscious paragon as to how he too would face the end.

Then there was the second sister. Patients, for her, were "sheer torture." A lovely, quiet, shy, and plain woman, she would drive herself mad experiencing her patients' pain, apologizing to a woman whom she knew would die painfully for her poor health and the futility of science in general. She understood horses, households, medicine—and yet knew she was fated to be alone. "She dearly loves," Chekhov explains, "family life, and though fate has denied her one of her own, she nonetheless seems to yearn for it."

Ronald Hingley dismisses the summer spent in Lika as less influential than those summers in Babkino (Hingley, 101). Indeed,

Babkino is, at least in terms of landscape, more closely linked to Chekhov's works, especially *The Cherry Orchard*. The more refined Kiselevs of Babinko were certainly more specific models for Chekhov's detailed portrayal of the upper classes in his plays. But the Lintarevs were Chekhovian in soul. Of the second Lintarev sister, Chekhov observed, "I can't imagine she has ever done anyone any harm, and I have the feeling she has never been and never will be happy for a single moment" (Karlinsky, 102). The Lintarevs were good people, but thwarted, exactly the type of character to which he would return obsessively. Such people make up the majority of Chekhov's most heartbreaking creations—talented, compassionate, trapped. They are the three sisters, they are the frail lady with a lapdog. They are the sister Kleopatra in "My Life" who mourns, "(H)aven't I wasted my youth? ... I have the cravings of a human being, and I want to live ..." And no one of the Lintarevs personifies this melancholy more than the second sister. In her, in her careworn aspect, her longing for a family life, for love, is born the kernels of women like Kleopatra, Olga of the *Three Sisters*, and *Uncle Vanya*'s homely Sonya.

In 1888, while Chekhov was at Lika, his brother Nikolai died. Chekhov's new play *The Wood Demon* was a failure. In 1890, he took off across Siberia to visit the penal convict community of Sakhalin, with the intent of producing a serious work. The resulting *Sakhalin Island* remains a landmark in Russian penal studies. It was not the first time that he had suddenly taken off. Ever since his twenties, Chekhov was plagued by the need to wander. But this was an adventure of an unprecedented caliber. Perhaps the urge to see Siberia was spurred by the knowledge that his days were limited; his tubercular attacks had increased in frequency and in violence in the past year. He returned from Sakhalin (which he dubbed Hell) via Ceylon (which he called Paradise) and Hong Kong, and was in Moscow only briefly before taking off for France and Italy. The next year he would settle himself, his parents, and his sister Mariya in an estate at Melikhovo, where they would reside for four years—the longest period that the adult Anton Chekhov would stay still.

The period after the return to Russia would be the most fruitful for Chekhov's short story writing. At no other period, are Chekhov's workaholic tendencies more in evidence. He wrote several of his major stories in rapid succession, while also working on *Sakhalin Island*. The Melikhovo estate needed intense renovation, and Chekhov threw himself vigorously into the tiring role of landowner, harvesting crops and planting trees. He wrote vaudeville plays to make ends meet and finished the seminal story "Ward Six." Remember that his health was not good. Remember, too, that he was still a doctor. It was a famine period in Russia, and Chekhov was deeply involved with relief work. At Melikhovo, he was named the district's "cholera superintendent," and between fighting starvation and epidemics, he found himself often begging money off of the local gentry. Apparently, he does not remember the sentry in the fondest of lights. In the 1892 story "My Wife," peasants lay dying while the pedantic, self-righteous narrator gluts himself with white suckling pig with horseradish and sour cream; then a rich, boiling hot cabbage soup with pork and buckwheat gruel ... pie ... pigeon stew, a kind of fried giblets, duck, partridge, cauliflower, fruit dumplings, curds and whey, and pancakes and jam to round it off.

As far as his writing was concerned, Chekhov's voice at this time is now confidently mature. The ghosts of Sakhalin are frequently in evidence, especially in "Ward Six." The lunatic conditions of a penal colony have metamorphosed into an actual asylum. It is, in the words of V. S. Pritchett, "one of the most intense, powerful, and claustrophobic (stories) he ever wrote." (Pritchett, 117) It is classic later Chekhov; in which the amorality of the tale is expressed by characters who expound their conflicting moral ideas without resolution. Dr. Ragin, a well-established doctor smug with success, discovers that the only intelligent member of his town is an inmate by the name of Gromov, in the insane asylum of which he is governor. Ultimately Ragin finds himself incarcerated in the same ward for insanity and beaten to death. It is a story, in Hingley's words, that points to the dangers of man's "non-resistance to evil." Ragin's eyes are open to the evils of Ward Six through his relationship with Gromov, and yet he does nothing. Appropriately, the evil to which he shuts his eyes ultimately claims him as a victim.

Nonetheless, "Ward Six" leaves me cold, as it did Chekhov, who called it "very dull." The characters talk too much. Monologues are lecture length. For example, Gromov expostulates:

> We are kept behind these bars, we're left to rot, we're given hell, but that is all spendidly rational because there's no difference between this ward and a warm comfortable study.

> Oh, it's a convenient philosophy, this is! You don't have to do anything, your conscience is clear, and you think yourself a sage.

Amazing, that a man who has been trapped behind bars with four lunatics and beaten regularly can still muster up the facility for complete sentences. What would have been genuinely sinister in the hands of a writer like Franz Kafka, loses its power because of the lengthy idealistic dialogue. There are, of course, the wonderful portraits of the other lunatics; there is Moses the Jew who "likes to be helpful"—bringing water to his fellow inmates, promising them new caps and kopecks, spoon-feeding his paralyzed neighbor. There is a bloated peasant, whom Chekhov refers to as a non-thinking, non-feeling "it"; when "it" is beaten, "it only rocks gently like a heavy barrel." There is an ex-post sorter who thinks he has been awarded the Order of St. Stanislaus. But such surreal horrors are submerged by the unbelievable eloquence of the two main characters. Ragin and Gromov are ideas, not men. There is definite irony in the story (Ragin dying in his own prison), but there is none of the typical Chekhovian lightness; there is little or no humanity. When Gromov dies, it is to make the story's point.

More successful, in my opinion, are the other stories that he wrote at the time. "Peasant Women," like "Ward Six" is resonant of Sakhalin. Chekhov, in his travels, encountered much of the awfulness that went on between the relationships amongst the poor. He saw shiploads of grey-faced convict women married hurriedly to convict men. Like "Ward Six," "Peasant Women" nowhere mentions Sakhalin by name, but evokes its desolation. It is a deformed, grotesque story—in its characters, setting, but also in its format. There is an innkeeper and a hunchbacked son. The women scuttle about, "ugly, wrinkled, tearstained." A man named Matvey arrives at the inn and tells the story of his mistress, who murdered her husband. He is defensive, corrupt, a monster of callousness. "I frightened the daylights out of her," he tells the innkeeper, "… you'll go to fiery Gehenna with all the other whores." After Matvey retires, the wife of the hunchbacked son urges her mother-in-law, "Let's kill Dyodya and Aloyshka!"

"Peasant Women" is a succinct story, uglier than the earnestly grim "Ward Six." The peasants in Chekhov's stories do not meditate upon their feelings—they act and shout and scream. It is not a physically violent story. Violence is reserved for dialogue. Women are sluts and cows who "get what they deserve"; men are "rotten bastards." There is an orphan boy, son of Matvey's mistress, hollow-cheeked and exhausted. Before leaving, the innkeeper and Matvey, who had just spent the last night in idle chit-chat, sling insults over the price of oats. Matvey's last words to him cement the story's anger. "I'll tear your ears off ... You little devil!"

The characters in "The Duel" are considerably more eloquent. As in "Ward Six," they moralize about life and fret about their angst. Yet while the debates in "Ward Six" are deeply serious, they are merely absurd in "The Duel." "The Duel" is a comedy, outrageously so, and populated by a wacky, yet beautifully delineated cast. There is the deacon who hangs out with this crowd because, like us, he finds them hilarious. There is the doctor Sarmoylenko, who is a cynic and yet wants to be good to everyone. Then there are Laevsky and Von Koren, and their ego-riddled rivalry. Von Koren is the ultimate scientist, the man who endorses Darwin's survival of the fittest. He's likeable because he is practically camp, preening in front of the mirror with his pistol. Instead of merely condemning Laevsky's behavior, he calls for Laevsky's annihilation. "Laevsky," he declares, "is as harmful and dangerous to society as a cholera microbe. Drowning him would be rendering it a service."

His nemesis Laevsky is the most popularly recurring of Chekhov protagonists; like Ivanov, and also like the heroes of "My Life" and "Three Years," he is the Russian Hamlet—harping ceaselessly about the death of love and the nature of ennui, torn between passion and indifference. But there is nothing romantic about Laevsky's brooding. In fact, "The Duel" is one of the few times in which the Hamlet character annoys us. What makes Laevesky different from someone like Ivanov is imperceptible. One suffers and the other whines—yet what they say is not all that different. This is what is magical about the best of Chekhov. He can take the same situations and personalities, tweak them a fraction, and completely flip our attitudes. As Chekhov's audience, we change our minds just as much as Chekhov's characters.

"The Duel" is similar in mood to Chekhov's later plays. It is as relentless in its banter as *The Seagull, Uncle Vanya, The Three Sisters*, and *The Cherry Orchard*. They talk, to paraphrase V. S. Pritchett, but they do not listen. It is interesting that after the failure of *The Wood Demon*, Chekhov began writing drama again in the 1890's., for he never considered himself a dramatist. Indeed, he said that he never could tolerate the theatre; the only thing that didn't bore him was one-act vaudevilles. That he is famous for his plays is interesting, for in his lifetime, he wrote only seven, and of those seven, only five of note. Compare this to his countless short stories. Indeed, his attitude towards play writing was remarkably prosaic; he said he liked *Ivanov* because each act closed like a story. In the end, there is not much difference between the short stories and the plays. In fact, Pritchett goes so far as to say that "his plays derive directly from his short stories," short stories that in Pritchett's mind, are "richer." (Pritchett, xi)

Whether or not this is a fair assessment is beyond the scope of this essay. But certainly Chekhov's public was not altogether supportive of his playwriting efforts, at least not at the beginning. *The Seagull* was a resounding failure when it opened in October 17, 1896; akin, as Callow says, "to one of Chekhov's farces." (Callow, 257). The star was a famous comic actress, E. I. Levkeeva, celebrating the twenty-fifth anniversary of her own debut. The audience was determined to laugh, and laugh they did. In the closing acts, laughter dissolved into hissing, and Chekhov fled. Compared to this fiasco, opening night for *Ivanov* was a flash in the pan. "I have witnessed a great many 'flops,'" wrote one theatre critic, "... but I can remember nothing resembling what happened at Levkeeva's 25th jubilee." It was, in fact, a perfect Chekhovian moment that a play about the theater should be such an onstage disaster, but Chekhov was too distressed to appreciate the irony. Like *Ivanov, The Seagull* is a comedy in which the hero shoots himself minutes before the curtain. It would be the last play in which there would be an important death. It would be the one play that specifically addresses the problems of creative achievement, the ways in which artists consume each other to survive.

In *The Seagull*, young writer Constantine Treplev finds himself the victim of his mother, the aging but great actress Irina Arkadina. In the play's opening scene, Constantine stages a play, and before it can get much underway, Irina is mocking it. After Constantine, furious, aborts the performance, she rants:

> I suppose he put on this performance, not as a joke, but to prove a point. He wanted to show us how to write and act ... I'm not annoyed. I'm only sorry to see a young man spend his time so tediously.

Irina is the classic mother-as-monster figure. As an actress, she lives with flamboyance. In the words of her son:

> She can cry her eyes out, reel off Nekrasov's poems by heart, and when it comes to nursing the sick she's quite the ministering angel.

As an actress, too, she craves attention and is one of the most selfish creations to have ever graced the stage. "The idea," Constantine explains, "is that we write about her, make a great to-do and rave about her marvelous acting ..." Irina confuses us, however, because we cannot condemn her. She genuinely loves Constantine as much as she hates him. She puts down the young Nina, not only because Nina is a young actress, but also because Nina is a rival for Constantine's affection. We are therefore sorry that she ages; sorry that she is trapped in the country with a sulky son; sorry that she doesn't have the audience that she deserves. But it is not just these sympathetic qualities that make us feel for Irina; ultimately, it is because she is so madly magnetic. There are two audiences to whom Irina plays—one onstage, the other off. She captivates them both. Hence, Irina Arkadina is a success; it is guaranteed that we will always pay the most attention to her. The only other character who can match Irina's charisma is her lover, the poet Trigorin. As an artist, too, his brilliance is on par with hers. And Trigorin is searching for his own prey. He finds it in Nina, whom he seduces, impregnates, and abandons.

There is hilarity in *The Seagull*, of a more barbed variety than in *Ivanov*. The romantic tangle (Constantine loves Nina, who loves Trigorin; Madvenko loves Masha, who loves Constantine, Arkadina lusts after Trigorin, loves Constantine, and loves herself) is madcap. Unrequited love is an absurdity. "Your loving me is all very touching," says the black-clad Masha to Madvenko, inhaling a pinch of snuff, "but I can't love you back and that's that." But nothing is funnier than Constantine's play. Nina sits on a boulder in the center of the stage:

> It is cold, cold, cold. Empty, empty, empty. Terrible, terrible, terrible. (Pause) The bodies of living creatures have turned to dust, and eternal matter has converted them into stones, water, clouds. But their souls have all been fused into a single whole. That World Spirit am I. I.

This must be one of the best send-ups of Symbolism that the theatre has ever witnessed. "Your play," Nina says, "is hard to act. There are no living people in it … There's not much action, just a lot of speeches."

Constantine is the most Hamlet-like of Chekhov's Hamlets, at least on the surface—he even recites Shakespeare's bedroom scene with Irina. He has the complicated mother, complicated relationship, and the usual score of complexes. In Act Two, when Constantine lays the seagull he shot that morning by Nina's feet, we assume that Nina will be the seagull; like Ophelia she will be sacrificed by Constantine in order to perpetuate himself. We are wrong. Constantine is unable to consume anyone, so he kills himself instead. It is not just because he is as cruel or powerful as Irina and Trigorin; it is because he is not as good an artist. In *The Seagull*, the best artists do make the best predators in the end.

Perhaps Chekhov would have never written another play had it not been for Stanvislavsky's restaging in 1896 of *The Seagull*, which would also bring Chekhov in contact with Olga Knipper, the woman who would eventually become his wife. Stanivslavsky's production was an unqualified success. *Uncle Vanya* and *The Three Sisters* followed. Of all of Chekhov's major works, *The Three Sisters* is the only one that is labeled as a drama, but *Uncle Vanya* is the one that is the most heartbreaking. Loneliness and restlessness are interwoven throughout the texts of both; but the central theme in both plays is that of thwarted lives, resonant, perhaps, of the days Chekhov spent at Luka with the Lintarevs. Indeed, in many ways, the three sisters in the play resemble the Lintarev sisters, in that they are talented, hard-working, stuck at their estate, and beholden to a feckless, well-meaning, but none-too-intelligent brother. They are, especially Masha, madly attractive. Sometimes they are given to poetic fits. But unlike the Lintarev sisters, they are not especially tragic. Says Irina,

> As far as we three girls are concerned, there hasn't been any
> beauty in our lives so far, life has been choking us like weeds
> in a garden.

But really, their lives do not seem so bad. They live on a beautifully appointed estate, and their house is always filled with a steady stream of soldiers and ardent suitors. "How I envy you!" says the lieutenant Vershinin. True, their brother gambles too much and plays a cuckold to his wife, and they long to be in Moscow, not in this provincial backwater.

Olga wishes that she had married, Masha wishes that she hadn't, and fresh, sparkling Irina doesn't really know what she wants. But even at the end of the play, when they are forced to leave their home, life does not seem quite so hopeless. They each have, as their brother points out, their own annuity. Irina will probably find herself in her beloved Moscow.

Should we feel sorrow? Or should we, as we do with many Chekhovian characters, pity them but recognize their self-indulgence? Masha may be unhappy in her marriage, but at least there will always be someone else to woo her, which is more than most unhappily married women can say for themselves. Indeed, there's really nothing to stop her from having an affair; after all, her sister-in-law Natasha does so right under her husband's nose. It is more the fear of crassness, I think, than of cruelty that prevents Masha from being a loose woman. Nor is there anything that really keeps Irina from Moscow, or from chasing her romantic dreams. She has enough money, and mountains of beauty and talent. There are people who are too sick, too anxious, too homely, or too poor to be happy. What restrains Irina, perhaps, is the knowledge that she is too spoiled to be happy.

Uncle Vanya, staged two years before in 1899, is more despairing. *Vanya* was based on *The Wood Demon*, a flop that Chekhov wrote more than ten years before and had rewritten in secret. Here we truly have wasted, hopeless lives. None of the *Three Sisters* seem to need work—rather, it gives them something to do; they are also too surrounded by luxury and suitors to be capable of real longing. Unlike *The Three Sisters*, *Vanya's* central characters are propelled by an urgent need to work and a genuine craving for love. What the three sisters take for granted is what the characters in *Vanya* most ardently desire. And yet the characters of *Vanya* complain less. Life is genteel, but shabbier than in the sunlit, party-filled house of *The Three Sisters*. There is, with *Uncle Vanya*, more of a kinship with the sad, noble Lintarev sisters.

One should begin with the least tragic characters first. Heading the Vanya household is the professor Serebryakov, old and loveless, but at least he is successful, has a daughter who loves him, and a wife who, though she does not, is at least young and gorgeous. Like Masha, Yelena married because she was in love with a man's mind. She is idle. "She does nothing," complains the doctor Astrov, "but eat, sleep, go for walks and enchant us with her beauty." Sonya tells her, as she might Irina or Masha if she knew them, "You're bored, you don't know what to do with yourself, and boredom and idleness are infectious." People are cruel to Yelena—out of envy, perhaps, or out of feelings of rejection. Yet we are hardly sorry for her. Hers is still a life of choice; Vanya, Astrov, and doubtless countless other men have proffered their hearts to her. She even wins the affection of her stepdaughter Sonya. Uncle Vanya says, "There's mermaid's blood flowing in your veins. So go on, be a mermaid." But boredom prevents her. Yelena is never more admirably sketched than in her final scenes with Astrov; ostensibly she is pleading on the behalf of Sonya, and yet there is that flicker of pleasure when she realizes he craves her. She flirts. "You're a sensible man, you can understand. It's even made me blush."

Astrov is another character who attracts us, and yet our pity for him is stifled. He is brilliant, observant, charismatic. Astrov talks at the longest length in the play, and there is always someone hanging upon his every word.. He too is blessed with choices. Astrov enjoys putting himself through hell. Therefore he drinks, he lets himself dwell on the one patient that he allowed to die under chloroform. He falls in love with Yelena, enjoying the tug between passion and indifference. When Astrov kisses Yelena for the last time, Chekhov instructs him to kiss her with nonchalance, for he has already moved on.

The truly melancholy characters are Sonya and her Uncle Vanya. Sonya is cursed with homely looks, and like the second Lintarev daughter, dreams of domestic idylls. She loves Astrov, her father, and even Yelena passionately, with no hope of it being returned on the same scale. "Oh, how dreadful," she sighs, "not to be beautiful." Ultimately, the power in Uncle Vanya's universe is centered in female beauty. Yelena has it and it mesmerizes with almost supernatural power; even Sonya is propelled towards it. Vanya calls Yelena a mermaid; Sonya calls her a witch. Sonya's diligence and good works do her no good in the end, especially because she dreams of love. Instead, she takes on the housekeeping duties, ministers to the poor, and shoulders the pain of the household. Sonya's need to work is more intense than in *The Three Sisters*; she works because she has to fill an empty heart. One has the impression that she is always pacing and never sleeping; no matter what hour of the night it is in a scene, Sonya is awake.

Her Uncle Vanya has thrown his life away for love. "You should have done something," his mother chides him. It is not the love of a woman, however; it is the love of a brother. He says, "I used to idolize that miserable, gout-ridden professor—worked my fingers to the bone for him ... He was the very breath of life for me." He is constantly declaiming his current hatred of his brother now; and yet when his brother proposes to sell the estate that has tied him down, Vanya goes mad. After all, he is being abandoned by those for whom he has wasted his life. He is forced to leave this estate over which he has slaved. In *The Three Sisters*, the characters long to be freed. Uncle Vanya dreads freedom. He has little now, but once he is freed, he will be an elderly man with nothing.

Comedy in *Vanya* is meant to be played broadly, and yet somehow the antics only underscore the poignancy. The clucking old nanny Marina usually gets a laugh from the outrageously material nature of her observations. Astrov asks her if he has changed. He demands, of course, the kind of reply that will be fodder for his angst. Instead, Marina says, "You were young and good-looking then, but you're beginning to show your age now and your looks aren't what they were either. Another thing, you like your drop of vodka." It becomes obvious, however, that Marina is the keystone to the others' sanity. They trouble themselves with problems of the heart and the mind; Nanny cures them with lime-flower tea.

Then there is the magical moment when Vanya shoots at the professor and fails. Such moments are the stuff of slapstick; gunshots, screeching wife, and no dead bodies at the end. The hilarity makes the scene exquisitely painful. Vanya tries to do a bold deed and looks ridiculous. There is no death in *Uncle Vanya*; for death—his own or his brother's—would have provided Vanya with release. It would have even made him into a hero, crystallized his "gifted, intelligent, courageous" potential. Indeed the characters of Sonya and Vanya, in Chekhov's work, arguably come closest to real tragedy. Sonya's closing words read like a memorial to the saintly, defeated few:

> We shall live through a long succession of days and endless evenings. We shall bear patiently the trials fate has in store for us. We shall work for others—now and in our old age—never knowing any peace. And when our time comes, we shall die without complaining.... And we shall find peace.

While *The Seagull*, *Uncle Vanya*, and *The Three Sisters* all deal with the gentry, the stories that Chekhov was writing around the same time teem with shopkeepers, house painters, and above all, peasants. While Chekhov may not have had the nicest things to say about the aristocracy, his lower class characters are violent, mercenary, hungry brutes. Gone are the pastoral hues that shaded earlier works like "Agafya" and "The Huntsman."

Superstition abounds. Chekhov cynically observes that "the richer they [the peasants] were, the less they believed in God." So it is poverty, more often than not, that breeds devoutness. Chekhov himself was a-religious; like the hero in "Three Years," he developed a deathly fear of religion because of his fanatic father. In "Murder," Matvei Terekhov is killed by his family. Matvei's cousin is a man who believes "that man cannot live without religion," who reads and sings and prays throughout the day, observes every fast with vigor, and conducts services at home because he believes the local church to be tainted. Even so, Chekhov cannot resist hinting at the hypocrisy of his practices; for they are "not for the sake of receiving blessings of some sort from God, but for the sake of good order." The ultimately murderous anger that the cousin feels for Matvei is fueled by the fact that Matvei, though richer, is staying with him, and rightly so, because Matvei owns half his tavern. Nonetheless, the cousin is able to give murder a holy justification. Ultimately, Matvei is killed because he insists on putting oil on his potatoes during a Lenten fast. Bloodlust and religion go hand in hand with results that are as hilarious as they are horrific:

> (Aglaia) uttered a shriek, snatched up the bottle of Lenten oil and with all her force brought it down straight on the skull of the cousin she hated ... Yakov, breathing heavily, excited, and feeling pleasure at the gurgle the bottle had made, like a living thing, when it struck the head, kept him from falling.

These people are capable of scalding a baby to death with a ladleful of hot water, as does the merchant daughter-in-law Aksynia of "In the Ravine." Men beat and insult; women sleep around. Fyokla of the marvelously impressionistic "Peasants" enjoys her country life; deceiving her husband with the workers on the river banks, splashing through puddles, eating and toiling with vigor. And yet she finds herself at the mercy of the local village brutes, and is sent home naked and shivering. This is gritty stuff, but not without beauty.

> (Fyokla) was shivering with cold, her teeth were chattering, and in the bright moonlight she looked very pale, strange, and beautiful. The shadows on her, the moonlight on her skin, stood out vividly, and her dark eyebrows and firm, youthful bosom were defined with peculiar distinctness.

Is it possible for the lower classes to exist nicely with the others? Chekhov seems to think not. In "New Villa," a well-to-do engineer's family takes over an estate and tries to assume the role of benevolent landowners. They build a bridge, they offer to help with the schools. It is the peasants who resist. "We've lived without a bridge," they repeat, "and we don't want one."

Two weeks after *Three Sisters* was staged in 1901, Chekhov married Olga Knipper. It is typical of Chekhov not to marry until at the cusp of his death, for Chekhov was famous for his ambivalence about sex. His heroes may have made love and enjoyed talking about it, but Chekhov's affairs were infrequent and private. Before Olga, there were the famous three Lydias—Lydia Yavorsky, Lydia Avilov, Lydia—or Lika—Mizinov. Of the three, he slept only with Yavorsky. But Avilov would write a turgid account claiming that she alone was the great love of Chekhov's life. Lika, a queenly ash-blonde, pursued Chekhov for years. By all accounts, the Lydias were not the only women in his life. He was an attractive man, stunning in his youth, and many women found him irresistible. In him was combined an honest appreciation of female attractiveness, ruthless intellect, and also a softness that made men like Leo Tolstoy exclaim that he was "Modest and quiet as a young lady!" (Smith, 1).

Above all, Chekhov was a man who understood the many dimensions of sexual attractiveness. In his writing, there are the strangely "pathetic," barely developed sylphs, such as the lady with a lapdog, Anna Seregyvena, whose conversation is marked with "diffidence and angularity," with her "slender weak neck, her beautiful grey eyes." There is the classical, fetching siren of "Ariadne." There are the women who are ugly, old, and yet simmering, such as the one who captures the heart of the hero in "Volodya." But there is surely nothing more lyrical, or astute, than the description of the young Russian girl in "The Beauties":

> … only her fair, wavy, thick hair could be called beautiful.
> Everything else was either irregular or very ordinary … She
> talked and laughed, displaying surprise and horror in turn
> and I can't recall a single moment when her body and face
> were still. The whole mystery and magic of her beauty lay in
> these tiny, infinitely refined moments … She had a butterfly-
> like beauty which goes hand in hand with waltzing, with
> fluttering about the garden, with laughter and gaiety, which
> is far removed from seriousness, sadness, and calm.

In short, Chekhov writes like a great lover. But in his life, he viewed sex as messy. Upon rising from a hotel bed with Yavorsky, he reflected, "… whatever form the 'unearthly bliss' of room 5 had taken, it had not been a prolonged sensual orgy." (Hingley, 188). He preferred, like *Uncle Vanya's* Astrov, to pine. As Olga Knipper would discover, he was not the easiest of lovers. They had fallen in love in 1896, and yet it took five more years of tearful ultimatums before he would finally agree to marry her. Yet Chekhov enjoyed the company of women, and was a fantastic flirt. He liked to maintain teasing correspondences, notably with Lika Mizinov, to whom he used to sign off with tantalizing phrases such as "Vanquished by you." In this regard, he might have had something in common with Gurov, the hero of "Lady with a Lapdog."

> When he was among women he felt at ease. He knew what
> to talk about with them and how to behave … There was
> something attractive, something elusive in his appearance, in
> his character and his whole person, that women found
> interesting and irresistible; he was aware of it, and was
> himself drawn to them by some irresistible force.

In his work, Chekhov demonstrates a keen eye for predatory women, as any man who was as often preyed upon as he was should. There are vampires like Ariadne, there are pretentious bits of fluff like Olga Ivanova in the hilarious "The Grasshopper." Then there is the other predatory woman, the kind who adopts the personality of the men that she loves—Olga Plemyannikov in "The Darling." (Not surprisingly, both of Olga Plemyannikov's husbands die young.) As different as these three women are, they are all, to a certain extent, actresses. Chekhov was, as his biographers tell us, both fascinated and repulsed by women of the theater. He felt their magnetism. After all, the only two women we can definitely link him with sexually were actresses. Yet he had a terror of their ability to pretend. On that note, however, while there is no predator more powerful or nuanced than Irina Arkadina, it is interesting to observe that Irina, the professional actress, is truer than Ariadne and the two Olgas, who act out their everyday lives. Perhaps Chekhov was not frightened of actresses, per se, but by the actress in every woman.

There are no happy marriages in Chekhov, but then again, there are no happy love affairs either. While adultery is as common in his world as cabbage soup, it is tedious when it lasts. If anything, such affairs are more depressing than marriage because they had originated in love. In Laevsky's words:

> As for love, I must inform you that life with a woman who's read Spencer and gone to the ends of the earth for you is just about as boring as living with any village girl. There's that same old smell of ironing, face powder and medicine, the same curling papers every morning, the same self-deception.

The only romantic affairs are those that are aborted by fate.

Such is the attitude that leads many critics to accuse Chekhov of being a misogynist. But no misogynist is able to paint feminine portraits with his subtlety. Indeed, Chekhov loved the women in his life. He might have been sexually wary, but the two people most important to him were his sister and his mother. In his writing, he demonstrates a delicate, almost surgical understanding of womanly nature. Each Chekhov woman is unique, perhaps even more so than the men. In "The Duel," Nadezkha is a better realized character than her lover Laevsky. She may be trifling and vain, yet she is able to inspire pangs. Lovingly, Chekhov details her oscillations. One moment, she thinks that there is "only the young, pretty, cultured woman in the town—herself." Another moment, she is pestered by "muffled hollow whispers, telling her she was a petty-minded, vulgar, worthless, insignificant woman." And nothing is more wrenching than when Laevsky tells her that she is a "tart," or when her neighbor criticizes her dress sense as "pretentious and gaudy." At such times, Nadezkha's shame becomes an enormous, pounding presence; her embarrassment is so painful it makes us want to avert our eyes.

Similarly, we do not despise Irina Arkadina, because she is so spectacular, running as she does through the gamut of emotions, and not all of them selfish. Even with a femme fatale like Ariadne we check ourselves. For Ariadne is described to us by a Hamlet figure almost as irritating as Laevsky. Shamokhin is handsome, intelligent, and wealthy, but hasn't the will to live, let alone make proper love. One character calls him an "old man at twenty-eight." When Ariadne tries to kiss him, he pleads, "These caresses without love make me unhappy!" Is Ariadne really as frigid as Shamokhin claims? Or is it a mythology he creates to justify his own inertia? Small wonder that Ariadne ill-treats him when she does.

In 1898, however, Chekhov published the moodily romantic "About Love." It is a tale of a thwarted affair, yet there is more sorrow than in the other Chekhov stories on the subject. Essentially a story within a story, the hero Alekhin tells his two friends how he and his good friend's wife fell in love. Neither declares it, as, in Alekhin's words, "we were afraid of everything that might reveal our secret to ourselves." (Incidentally, Lydia Avilova, always on the lookout for evidence for Chekhov's devotion, pounced on this story with joy, for she was married to Chekhov's friend.) Under the strain of silence, the two become cold and angry. Love is expressed too late. The wife departs on a train. Then there is the last sentence. Alekhin has finished his story. The rain clears. The listeners, it seems, know the woman involved, and Chekhov ends, "Both of them had met her in the town, and Burkin knew her and thought her beautiful." It is an ending that would not reverberate with the power with which it does if the story itself were not so sad. This is Chekhov at his best, conveying feeling through description, not explanation. It leaves us at a loss to analyze what has touched us so much.

Was Chekhov getting soft? For most of his characters are not in love as much as falling out of it. But "About Love" is a story that addresses the painful thing itself. "The Lady with A Lapdog" goes one step further, for love at the end is still not thwarted. This is a simple tale of adultery one Yalta summer. For the woman, it is her first affair; for the man, it is one of many summer adventures. But they fall in love nonetheless, and at the end, they stay that way. For Chekhov himself has fallen in love—with Olga Knipper. Like the hero Gurov,

> It was only now, when his hair was beginning to turn grey, that he had fallen in love properly, in good earnest—for the first time in his life.

There is nothing immediately fascinating about Gurov's beloved, Anna Sergavenya. In fact, she strikes the well-versed seducer as "pathetic." And yet when they are separated, he hears "her breathing, her dress rustle." She has infiltrated him entirely. Yet "Lady with a Lapdog," as does "About Love," escapes sentimentality. For in Chekhov, love is a thing that is simply expressed. He writes, "[They] loved each other as people do who are very dear and near, as man and wife or close friends who love each other." In certain ways, we are returned to the Chekhov who moved us so deeply in "Misery." And yet the love in this story is not easy. It is fascinating that Chekhov, who had suffered so much in his life, found so much agony in the comparatively trivial anxieties of romance. Olga was acting in Moscow, and the lovers, like Gurov and Anna, had to wait months before they could meet. This, for Chekhov, was a new sort of ache. The closing sentence of "Lady with a Lapdog" is among Chekhov's most famous:

> And it seemed to them that in only a few more minutes a solution would be found and a new, beautiful life would begin, but both of them knew very well that the end was still a long long way away and that the most complicated and difficult part was only just beginning.

Gurov and Anna tell themselves they are on the brink of beauty, even when they know the hopelessness ahead. Self deception is still necessary for the endurance of love, but now Chekhov no longer derides it. Such a sentence is one that Callow calls "a masterful moment." (Callow, 287). It is extraordinary because it is one of the purest threads ever spun from the human heart.

But marriage to Olga was not all roses. She refused to give up her acting career, and the couple continued to see each other almost as rarely as they had before the wedding. Chekhov had been forced to move to Yalta for his health, and Olga was installed in an apartment in Moscow. Frequently, he pleaded for her to come home, but more often than not, his companions remained his sister and mother. Olga miscarried, but the baby was most likely fathered by another man. Meanwhile, although he had been hospitalized a number of times, Chekhov had still not stopped the itinerant life; he shuttled to Europe, to Petersburg, and to Moscow to see his wife. *The Cherry Orchard* was his last play.

It would be a return to the theme of restlessness. This time, however, the abandonment of *Vanya* and the longing for escape in *Three Sisters* are combined. The characters are torn between the need of a home and the need to forget themselves by traveling. *The Cherry Orchard* is a play inspired by the bankruptcy of the Kiselevs, the family that owned Babinko, where young Chekhov used to summer. It opens as a homecoming. Mrs. Ranevsky and her daughter return from Paris, where Mrs. Ranevsky has been trying to forget the death of her young son. From the beginning, we know that her estate, the cherry orchard, is for sale. At the end, it is bought by the nouveau riche Lopakhin, and Mrs. Ranevsky is on the road again.

There is no bliss waiting for the characters at the end. Whatever happiness Mrs. Ranevsky and Anya experience abroad, as Michael Frayn points out, will endure only as long as their wallets. (Frayn, lxviii) Says Mrs. Ranevsky, "I'll live on the money your great aunt sent from Yaroslavl to buy the estate—good old Aunty! Not that it will last very long." When the money runs out, so will their contentment. Yet *The Cherry Orchard* is Chekhov's truest comedy. The characters are aristocrats to an extreme, supercilious and naïve. We like them, but we can't feel sorry for them. They embody creamy charm, especially Mrs. Ranevsky, as she descends from her carriage, hands outstretched and tears in her eyes, followed by a German governess and a trotting little dog. "The nursery!" she exclaims, "My lovely, heavenly room! I slept in here when I was a little girl. And now I feel like a little girl again." Everyone calls each other "angel" and "terribly sweet." And of course what is evident from the beginning is that despite their lyrical reminiscences, they don't really care about their cherry orchard. At the end of Act 3, Mrs. Ranevsky is weeping, but then again, she's always weeping. Besides, what upsets her is not the orchard's sale, but the sale of the orchard to Lopakhin, whom she considers—despite her democratic pretenses—to be the wrong man. Besides, Mrs. Ranevsky makes a remarkable recovery. "I'm not so much on edge," she says, quaffing champagne before the final curtain, "And I'm sleeping better."

It is as if Chekhov was mocking himself as he wrote this play, trivializing his angst by hanging it on the lips of Mrs. Ranevsky. Also interesting is that this purest of comedies should be written by a dying man. Chekhov would die on July 2, 1906, in Badenweiler, Germany, six months after *The Cherry Orchard*'s premiere. It must be said that he was in denial of his condition. But as the end drew nearer, he only grew lighter. In his personal life, he was given to cracking jokes. "It could be said of you and me," he wrote to Gorky, another consumptive, "that two authors had spent a fine evening together having an interesting cough together" (Callow, 396). In his last few months, he insisted on being entertained by visitors. And his deathbed scene, one of the most famous in literary history, was exquisitely in keeping with his style. Chekhov's German doctor, usually so rule-abiding, summoned the hotel for three cut-crystal glasses and a bottle of the hotel's best champagne. It was after midnight, and the porter was tousled. Chekhov emptied his glass with a smile and the words, "It's been a long time since I've had champagne." For the very last time in his life, he had refused a tragic ending.

VIRGINIA LLEWELLYN SMITH

Love

If we seek to clarify Chekhov's attitude to love, we are immediately confronted, as in so many other aspects of his life, with ambiguity. What is by no means certain is that Chekhov, during those years when Lika, Avilova—and perhaps other women—hoped to win his heart, was actively seeking to fall in love with anyone. True, he wrote to Suvorin in October of 1892: '... I wouldn't at all object to falling in love. It's a dull life when you're not madly in love'; and to Elena Shavrova in 1896: 'You write that you want fame much more than love; and I the contrary: I want love much more than fame.' But these words cannot be taken entirely at face-value: they are unmistakably tinged with the bantering tone into which Chekhov so readily fell in his correspondence.

He could go further and be downright cynical. In 1896 Suvorin noted in his diary the following sentiments, under a general heading, 'Some of Chekhov's ideas': 'Friendship is better than love. My friends are fond of me, I am fond of them, and through me they are fond of one another. Love makes enemies of those who love the same woman. When in love, men wish to possess a woman entirely, to let no one else have her, and they consider anyone who conceives the urge to attract her as their enemy. Friendship knows no such jealousy. For that reason friendship is better than love, even in marriage.'

From *Anton Chekhov and the Lady with the Dog*. © 1973 by Oxford University Press, pp. 126-142. Reprinted by permission.

Now, despite the unequivocal tone, these words do not mean that Chekhov was uninterested in love, and they need not invalidate attempts to find a love-object in Chekhov's past. Only two years later, Chekhov, as we have seen, urged his younger brother Misha in equally direct language to remember the supreme importance of love in marriage. A sudden *volte-face*? Perhaps. But the same sober, apparently so rational tone in which Chekhov puts friendship before love in 1896 had been heard before: in 1888 he wrote to his elder brother Aleksandr: 'You ... know perfectly well that family-life, music, caresses, fond words, aren't to be had by marrying the first woman you come across, even if she is a decent girl, but by *love*.'

A fluctuating attitude, indeed. Yet not for a moment need we doubt Suvorin's accuracy when he set down the contrary opinion as Chekhov's. For upon examination of the theme of love in Chekhov's fiction, it will be seen that the existence of love-friendship side by side with love-passion was for Chekhov a fundamental and fascinating fact of life.

'Friendship is better than love.' The remark is intriguing on several counts. Perhaps most of all because it sounds like the comment of a man who has never been passionately in love. Most men (and women) would after all find natural the typical lover's less than altruistic attitude, of which Chekhov here speaks so disparagingly. That he should do so suggests that he was clinging to an abstract ideal of love, based on no experience that can have approximated to the typical lover's sexual passion. The insight is hypothetical, but it is reinforced by the recollection that sexual jealousy plays only a very minor role in Chekhov's fiction.

Aside from his jocular remarks quoted above, which one must hesitate to take literally, there are scarcely any references in the whole of Chekhov's correspondence which suggest that he personally wanted to fall in love. However, as in his dealings with female admirers, so in other matters Chekhov was adept at concealing what he really thought, whether he did so by being facetious or by keeping silent. Thus there is some justification for the speculation of critics who say that Chekhov was dreaming of '*un grand amour romantique*' or talk of his 'hunger for love'. Certainly, Chekhov's general pronouncements on love—those which were not intended to be taken as a comment on his personal affairs—show that he took love very seriously. Even more significant than the homilies addressed to his brothers are a couple of lines written in 1889 to Suvorin—towards whom Chekhov felt no such strong pontificatory urge: 'Love is no joke. If people shoot themselves because of it, it means they take it seriously, and that's important.' The earnest tone of this comment suggests that Chekhov had stronger views on the subject of love than his correspondent might have suspected. In any case, at least one critic, H. P. Collins, is shown to have been badly misled when he writes: '[Chekhov's] marriage with the Alsatian actress Olga Knipper ... remains rather puzzling. Though in his later stories he wrote with increasing poignancy of frustrated love, the love for women seems to have had little serious part in his life.' The implication would seem to be that Chekhov somehow stumbled into marriage as he might have stumbled into a hole in the ground; and it is surely much more likely that Chekhov wrote poignantly about frustrated love because love did, in some sense at least, have a serious part in his life. Whether or not Chekhov dreamt for years of a great romantic love, he did experience love towards the end of his short life: and it was a love which we know he took seriously, because at this point Chekhov dropped his reticence. The evidence of his feelings is to be found throughout his correspondence, from the day he encountered the woman who was to become his wife.

2

Olga Leonardovna Knipper was in her late twenties when Chekhov made her acquaintance at a rehearsal of *The Seagull* on 9 September 1898. A month later, after seeing her play Irina in A. K. Tolstoy's *Tsar Fedor Ioannovich* he wrote from Yalta to Suvorin: '... best of all was Irina. If I'd stayed in Moscow I would have fallen in love with that Irina.'

In May of the following year Olga visited Chekhov at Melikhovo: after this, in June, their correspondence began. Chekhov's letters were full of the inevitable banter, but they also contained more than a suggestion of serious involvement. His second communication with her began: 'Hail, last page of my life....' Few phrases could provide a more substantial indication of Chekhov's desire for a permanent relationship.

In the summer of 1899 he and Olga stayed in Yalta, he at an hotel and she with friends. They travelled back to Moscow together in August, going over the Ai Petri range and through the Kokkoz valley together in a carriage. It was almost certainly on this journey, within less than a year after their first meeting, that they agreed to marry: for in a letter some months later Olga wrote, saying that she had heard that Chekhov was going to marry someone else: 'Congratulations, dear writer, so you couldn't hold out?'—and adding that she will come to upset his domestic tranquillity: 'After all, we came to an agreement—remember the Kokkoz valley?'

By late August of that year Chekhov was back in Yalta, settled in the south more or less permanently, while Olga was kept in the north by her work. The romance continued by correspondence. From the start, Chekhov's letters show an enormous enthusiasm for his love, which expressed itself in uninhibited affection: 'Hello, dear, precious wonderful actress! ... Hello, my joy!'

Olga came to Yalta on tour with the Moscow Arts Theatre in April 1900, and in July on a private visit to Chekhov. It was on this second visit that they apparently became lovers; for a switch from '*vy*' to '*ty*' in their correspondence began at this point.

The sexual side of Chekhov's relationship with Olga Knipper has already been discussed. The romantic side, as revealed in Chekhov's correspondence, was no less satisfactory for him. He was joking when he wrote to Olga in January of 1901: 'I wish you ... still more love, to last even longer, about fifteen years. What do you think, is love like that possible? For me it's possible, but not for you ...'; but his tone expresses his confidence in his new situation. Now that he had found a relationship in which he was free to do so Chekhov referred to his love repeatedly, even quite openly, in a telegram: '... well, in love....'

They married on 25 May 1901, and throughout the rest of their life together Chekhov continued to assure Olga of his devotion. 'Believe that I love you, love you profoundly,' he told her. 'Whatever might happen, even if you suddenly turned into an old hag, I'd still love you—for your soul, for your disposition.' 'No one in the world loves you as I do,' he told her on another occasion. And on another: 'My dear, good, splendid gifted little actress, God bless you, I love you very much.'

Although there is nothing particularly remarkable about the way in which Chekhov expressed his love, it is necessary to underline the written evidence of his affection for Olga Knipper, because a certain faction seems to regard Olga in her position as Chekhov's wife at best with surprise, at worst with animosity. For example: Collins, in the remainder of his article, implies that the marriage was entered into without love on Chekhov's part and with an uncomprehending attraction on Olga's; Chekhov's friend Bunin claimed that until he read Avilova's reminiscences—and believed her story—he had thought there to be no great love in Chekhov's life: which is as much as to say that Chekhov did not love Olga Knipper. The same is implied by Altshuller, Chekhov's doctor in Yalta, who wrote: '... when I read about [Chekhov's] especially "deep and tender" love for anybody, I think that one must take this in a very relative sense.' Other contemporaries and critics of Chekhov have voiced or implied their disapproval of Olga.[1]

Unfortunately this dislike is more graphically expressed than the reasons for it: but these seem fairly obvious. Olga herself took violently against certain people and could be a malicious enemy, as her letters to Chekhov show. Many must have been jealous of her, whether on account of her own success or her influence on Chekhov. Anyone who reads it in context will recognize the undertone of jealousy in Bunin's remark (relating to Easter 1901): 'Chekhov, even when Olga Leonardovna was there, insisted on my spending every day at his house.' Altshuller disapproved of Olga because he thought that her irruption into Chekhov's life ruined his patient's health. Similar feelings were no doubt entertained by others, less directly involved in Chekhov's well-being, who regarded Chekhov as society's, or Russia's, property rather than as master of his personal affairs. It is extremely interesting to note in this connection the far greater amount of interest and sympathy shown by most of Chekhov's contemporaries and biographers towards Lika Mizinova, which is out of all proportion to the interest Chekhov showed in her. This of course is partly due to the fact that Knipper was alive until 1959, whereas Lika was dead and her life history open to speculation and elaboration by 1937. It is also an excellent demonstration of the audience-appeal of unhappy love.

If the tone of Chekhov's letters to Lika suggests that he was fond of her, the tone of his letters to Olga puts it beyond doubt that he loved her very dearly. If further proof of this love be demanded, it can be found in the affection that Chekhov's sister Masha showed towards Olga Knipper. Masha Chekhova, as we shall see, was passionately devoted to the cause of her brother's well-being: and that she and Olga became lifelong friends in spite of the jealousy they felt for one another is conclusive proof that Chekhov's love for his wife was obvious to those who observed them together.

Olga Knipper can no more easily be equated with Chekhov's fictional romantic heroines than can his other women friends. Like most of these, and as one would indeed expect of the actresses among them, Olga was sociable and vivacious rather than timid and retiring. Like Lika, she became depressed and elated easily. She was ten years younger than Chekhov, but she was no adolescent when he met her. Her letters to Chekhov sometimes reveal a trait of immaturity—but not the kind of pure uncorrupted childlike vision that Chekhov depicted in his fiction. Olga's immaturity is revealed rather in a tendency to worry over trivial matters—and in a childish sense of fun, which she herself was the first to admit to: 'Do you remember taking me back as far as the stairs, and the stairs creaking so treacherously? I adored that. Heavens, I'm writing like a schoolgirl', she wrote to Chekhov with reference to the early stages of their love-affair.

It is not in fact particularly rewarding to speculate why Chekhov loved Olga. The important thing is that he believed that he had found love, and he once told her that the longer he lived with her, the broader and deeper his love would become. In being identified with Chekhov's concept of true love, Olga Knipper corresponds symbolically to the romantic heroine, even if not in other respects.

It was for Olga Knipper that Chekhov wrote the part of Masha in *Three Sisters*, one of Chekhov's finest creations and the last of his romantic heroines. 'Oh, what a part you've got in *Three Sisters*! What a part!' he told her as he was writing the play.

The charm of Masha as a character lies in her possessing both the 'poetic' attributes of the romantic heroine and a strong personality which can easily be 'put across' to the audience. Her part may be compared with the part of Nina Zarechnaya in *The Seagull*, which is very difficult to play well.[2] Nina's role is too dependent upon the symbolic significance which others are supposed to see in her. Her speaking-part does not bear the imprint of individuality, and so she fades into the symbolic pattern of her fate: beauty injured, hope triumphant.

By contrast, Masha's individuality is emphasized and the pattern of her fate, which also resolves itself into love-disappointment-hope, is toned down. Her personality is dramatized: she wears black; swears and whistles; is blunt to the point of rudeness; hot-tempered (she even snaps at her pathetic old nurse); her behaviour is moody, unpredictable and odd: she intends to leave before Irina's party, and then abruptly changes her mind; she is asleep during the fire scene while her sisters are in a state of great agitation; she is preoccupied and bursts into snatches of song. In a word, she is mysterious—different from her sisters. (And what is more, Chekhov intended her to be aware of this: in the confession scene, he told Knipper, Masha feels that she is more intelligent than her sisters.)

The drama of her love for and forced renunciation of Vershinin is, on the other hand, underplayed. Masha is shown not to feel bitter about her marriage to the absurd Kulygin: she speaks about it in a calm, matter-of-fact way: 'I'm used to him....' Vershinin's love for her is expressed in his highly emotional speech of Act 2: 'I love you, love you, love you ...' (there is nothing very subtle about the way he is depicted), but we do not finally know Masha's mind until Act 3, when the fact of their complete knowledge of one another is revealed in the interchange, meaningless to outsiders, 'Tram-tam-tam ... Tam-tam', etc. When Masha tells her sisters of her love, the scene is again underplayed: or should be, as Chekhov was at pains to point out to Knipper: 'it's not a confession at all, just a frank talk ... the main thing ... is to put across that it's been an exhausting night.' And at the climax of the play Masha's present grief—as is Irina's—is dominated by the question of the future: 'They're leaving us ... we're left alone, to begin our lives from the beginning again. Life must go on ...'—thus runs Masha's last speech.

This deliberate synthesis of the dramatic and the non-dramatic in the presentation of Masha does not sound subtle, but it is peculiarly effective on the stage. Masha's predicament, as befits a romantic heroine, is not devoid of pathos: 'When you take happiness in little snatches, bit by bit, and then lose it, you gradually become thick-skinned and bad-tempered', but never does she appear to be sentimentalized. The part played by Irina helps here. It is Irina who possesses, at first glance, the characteristics of the typical Chekhovian romantic heroine. In Act 1 Irina is dressed in white, filled with a childlike *joie de vivre*. Chebutykin 'poeticizes' her into a little girl; Tuzenbakh and Soleny poeticize her as the woman they love; although none of those people really know Irina: she has her symbol—the locked piano. But her sisters—and the audience also—see the unromantic side of her—see her as an ordinary girl, growing older and disillusioned as the years pass.

Irina however could be said to take over, to a certain extent, in place of Masha, the pure childlike aspects of the heroine which seem to have obsessed Chekhov. Masha is devoid of these characteristics, which are not always easy to put across sympathetically to audience or reader.

Masha is mature, and not 'pure', at least not in terms of conventional morality. She shocks her sister Olga by glorying in her love for another man. Yet Masha is the most 'heroic' of the play's three heroines, because it is she who chiefly represents true spiritual values, as Chekhov saw them. It is she who comes out with the strongest tirade against vulgarity, in Act 2; it is she who most sharply criticizes Natasha, the incarnation of vulgarity, before Natasha makes her appearance; she who expresses dislike of 'that Mikhail Potapych, or Ivanych'— Protopopov, who later becomes Natasha's lover. Conversely, she is attracted by idealism: after Vershinin's visionary monologue on the values of culture in an uncivilized world, she decides to stay to lunch after all. She falls in love with him: and, what is most important, her heightened sensitivity makes her the most aware of what love should be. She knows that Kulygin's expressions of devotion to her are as automatic, sterile, and intrinsically as meaningless as is the chanted paradigm of *amare* which she repeats in her irritation with him. She believes that love has tremendous importance: it places one in a different frame of experience, where all considerations are subject to the demands of love. 'When you read a novel, you think it's all old hat, and there's no mystery about it,' she tells her sisters, 'but when you fall in love yourself it becomes obvious to you that nobody knows anything, and everyone must take decisions for himself....'

Is it to Olga Knipper that we are indebted for this at one and the same time credible, interesting, and poetic heroine? Chekhov may well have endowed Masha with certain of Olga Knipper's traits, but there are no striking points of resemblance between Masha and what we know of Olga Knipper. Nor is it to be expected that there should be, for Chekhov created the role of Masha for Olga with the intention of providing her with a good part to play, rather than of portraying her character. Masha's personality, whomever it is derived from, is not the motivation of the play; *Three Sisters* contains themes, characters, and situations which Chekhov had used before; it was written as an experiment in dramatic technique, as were his other major plays. The credibility of both Masha and Irina as romantic heroines is due to Chekhov's increasing mastery of his dramatic technique.

3

All Chekhov's romantic heroines of the stage have an inherent advantage over their counterparts in his fiction: they have, when they are on the stage, a physical presence and cannot be shadowy or totally insipid. Moreover, the success of Chekhov's dramatic technique is mainly dependent upon sureness of characterization; to a lesser extent, on the creation of an atmosphere; to a still lesser extent on the plot, which tends in the case of Chekhov's major plays to be minimal and very simple.

The technique which Chekhov used in most of his love-stories is more conventionally dramatic. In these the plot is also simple, but it is much more important. We are presented with a schematic pattern: love is thwarted by extraneous circumstances, as in 'The Artist's Story' and 'About Love'; or the chance of finding love is thoughtlessly thrown away, as in 'Miss N.'s Story' (*Rasskaz gospozhi N.N.*, 1887) and 'Lights'; or love ends in disillusionment, as in 'The Story of an Unidentified Person' and 'The Teacher of Literature' (*Uchitel' slovesnosti*, 1894): this occurs when one of the partners is shown to be, or to become, a *poshlyak*. The essential feature of these works is what happens to love, and the actual nature of the love relationship is not investigated. We have, for example, in 'The Story of an Unidentified Person', the heroine, Zinaida Fedorovna, who is 'good', the villain, Orlov, who is 'bad': the action is set in motion by Zinaida Fedorovna's leaving her husband, and a gloomy *dénouement* inevitably follows. Like the narrator, we never really understand why Zinaida Fedorovna loves Orlov. Here the characters as individuals are interesting, but not in their relationship with one another, which remains mysterious. More frequently, only one partner is interesting at the other's expense—usually the heroine's.

The absence of an analysis of the *nature* of relationships between human beings—an omission perhaps imposed by the restrictions of the short-story form—is compensated for by atmosphere, which in the Chekhovian love-story is all-important: this type of story depends almost entirely for its effect on 'poetry'—on the ability of the reader to enter into a world of nostalgia and anguish and to find something in it which touches him personally. Chekhov's treatment of love relies heavily for its effect on sentences such as: 'What enormous happiness it is to love and to be loved, and how dreadful it is to feel that one is about to topple from this lofty tower!' ('My Life') or: '... at times when I feel melancholy and weary of solitude I have vague memories and gradually for some reason the idea takes hold of me that someone is remembering me too, and waiting for me, and that we shall meet.... Misyus, where are you?' ('The Artist's Story'). The effectiveness of Chekhov's love-stories depends upon our appreciating the mystique with which he surrounds love. That the romantic heroine is in danger of seeming insipid—unless Chekhov specifically makes a feature of her non-poetic aspects—is due to the fact that the heroic role is really played by love. Love, rather than any character, stands for the ultimate in desirability.

In the world of Chekhov's fiction love is regarded not merely as an embellishment of existence, but as indispensable to existence. 'Without love there would be no life; he who fears it and evades it is not a free man': the words are those of Dr. Blagovo in 'My Life', who has seduced Kleopatra, the narrator's sister. Blagovo is very sympathetically portrayed and the implication clearly is that the importance of love justifies his action. In 'About Love' it is again emphasized that love should take precedence over everything else: the climax of the story is reached when Alekhin, saying farewell to his beloved Anna whom he has never claimed, realizes that 'when you love someone, all considerations regarding your love must take as their starting-point something higher and more important than happiness or unhappiness, sin or virtue in their everyday sense, or else you must take nothing into consideration at all.'

These words would seem to sanction a dangerous egocentricity, were it not for the fact that idealized love is presented in Chekhov's work as a power for great good, even as a regenerative force. In the original published version of 'About Love' Chekhov wrote: 'When you love someone you discover such riches in yourself, such a bottomless well of tenderness and kindness, that you can scarcely believe you are capable of such love.' Later, he cut this sentence out, probably because such asides interfered with the pace of what is essentially a fast-moving narrative: but the idea is developed more fully in the many ways similar theme of 'The Lady with the Dog'. Gurov's love-affair with Anna Sergeevna inspires in him a feeling of disgust for the tenor of his day-to-day life: 'the frenzied card-playing, the gluttony, the drunkenness, the continual discussion of the same topics....' In 'The Artist's Story' there is an implicit contrast between the beauty of the artist's love for Misyus and the unromantic cohabitation of his host Belokurov with his pompous housekeeper who looks like a fatted goose. The weakness and cynicism of Chebutykin, the doctor in *Three Sisters*, is redeemed to a great extent by the one uplifting and ennobling feature of his character—his genuine and touching love for Irina. Andrei's love for Natasha, on the other hand, while it may strike us as touching, is not uplifting or ennobling, because, as we have seen, only by his excessive stretch of imagination is she a romantic heroine. For love in the world of Chekhov's fiction is only a great force for good when the loved one is worthy: the ideal of love demands an ideal love-object. So Chekhov would seem to be saying when he jotted in one of his notebooks: 'Love is a blessing. It is not for nothing, indeed, that at all times amongst practically all civilized nations love in the broad sense and the love of a husband for his wife are both alike called love. If love is frequently cruel and destructive, the cause of this lies not in love itself but in the inequality of human beings.' People, therefore, must live up to the concept of love.

Of no one more aptly than of Chekhov could it be said that 'the dramatist cannot afford to question the absoluteness of the emotions out of which his drama is concocted.' The critic who wrote these words was discussing Tolstoy the novelist, and he is making a point about the difference in this respect between Tolstoy's work and that of a dramatist. Tolstoy's treatment of love in his two greatest novels is markedly different from Chekhov's treatment of love within the 'dramatic' framework of his short stories, and it would seem apposite to indicate briefly the nature of the difference.

At the end of *War and Peace*, when Natasha Rostova, the romantic heroine *par excellence*, has changed into a fussy demanding matron, we may feel that her love and Pierre's has devolved into some more mundane emotion. But do we find Pierre kicking against the traces of domesticity, crying, like Chekhov's teacher of literature (in the story of that name): 'I must escape from here, escape this very day, or I'll go mad!'? Far from it. Similarly, in *Anna Karenina*, it is clear that the love of Kitty and Levin is not, and never has been, ideal and pure: in Kitty it originally contained an element of her fear of spinsterhood, and after marriage it is threatened by the evolution and alteration of emotions in both partners. This causes them, the protagonists, pain, but it is the author's vision which is dominant, and the author's vision remains in this connection serene: life and love are like that, Tolstoy knows it and he assumes that we realize it, whether we like it or not. There is no suggestion of anguish or irony. Tolstoy could adopt this attitude to changes in the nature of love because his novels, as far as the love-stories in them are concerned, have as their hero the family. Still with the same apparent detachment, Tolstoy leads the love-story of Anna Karenina herself to its conclusion of turmoil and tragedy. Anna neither can nor wishes to see her relationship with Vronsky devolve into peaceful domesticity. She has only the ideal of 'love' to cling to.

Significantly Chekhov, in his two essays in the novel genre, 'The Duel' and 'Three Years', was to examine relationships in evolution: the conclusions he came to in these isolated works will be discussed in a later chapter. But in by far the greater proportion of his fiction the view of love propounded is that of his favourite Anna Karenina herself: love has the immutable quality of the ideal.

In Chekhov's later work, this ideal of love was to become increasingly associated with the concept of something above and beyond the transient, or more precisely, with a quasi-philosophical speculative interest, and a quasi-mystical faith, in the future of mankind. In *Three Sisters*, Masha's relationship with Vershinin arouses our sympathy because it is a predicament of immediate 'human interest'; but we note that Masha is initially attracted to Vershinin by his idealistic vision of the future. There is no 'human interest' in the romance between Anya and Petya Trofimov in *The Cherry Orchard*, because it is devised merely as a prop to their interest in and ambition for the future; and the chance of making a dramatically poignant minor tragedy of the *romance manquée* of Lopakhin and Varya is made little of. This is because the plot-scheme of *The Cherry Orchard* is as follows: youth's innocent love and hope for the future is contrasted with their elders' corruption and nostalgia for the dying past. In 'Betrothed', Chekhov's last short story, and in which more than in any other there is a recognition of the social forces that were changing women's lives, there is a fusion of the social and the romantic theme—or rather, the lack-of-the-romantic theme, because Nadya does not love her fiancé: she does not love him because he is smugly content to regard his social inactivity as a 'sign of the times.' Even in 'The Lady with the Dog', in which the actual nature of the human relationship described is of paramount interest, the awakening of love forms a bridge to idealistic philosophizing: 'As he sat beside the young woman, who was looking so lovely in the dawn light, calmed and enchanted by the fairytale setting of the sea, the mountains, the clouds, the vast sky, Gurov thought how, if one came to think of it, essentially everything on earth was beautiful, everything save our own thoughts and deeds, when we forget the higher aims of existence and our human worth.'

This feeling of involvement with the future of mankind which Chekhov seems to be seeking to transmit in his late works is of course especially interesting when viewed in the light of subsequent events in Russia, and much has been written by both Soviet and Western writers on the development of the theme in Chekhov's work and its significance. On the basis alone of the optimistic outlook expressed by so many of Chekhov's characters one can challenge the view that Chekhov was a gloomy cynic which was held by many early critics of Chekhov, notably by Shestov.

But, however great Chekhov's interest in man's future may have been—and it is possible that the theme was introduced into his stories and plays only to uphold the theory expressed in one of his plays that 'a work of art must express some great idea', rather than that his stories and plays were to any extent inspired by the theme itself—love, in Chekhov's work, is not regarded as an emotion secondary or subordinate to sociological zeal or preoccupation with the future. Chekhov makes it clear, for instance, in *Three Sisters* that Irina Prozorova is not looking forward to happiness when she marries Tuzenbakh although she is to lead a 'new life' as a teacher. Why? Because she does not love Tuzenbakh, and she has made the sacrifice of the imaginary figure she calls her 'real' husband. There is no question in her view—or ours—of the new life being in any way a substitute for love. Nor, in *The Cherry Orchard*, is there any doubt as to who is meant to be the moral victor in the splendid clash of philosophy between puritanical Trofimov, who pompously declares himself to be 'above love' and the down-to-earth Ranevskaya: 'I am above love!' she reiterates in mockery. 'You're not above love, you're just ... half-baked.' The absurdity of Trofimov's position is promptly underlined by his falling downstairs. As for Ranevskaya, it is felt that if anyone's sins are to be forgiven on account of having loved much, hers will be.

Given his preoccupation with the subject of love, it is not surprising that Chekhov entitled one of his works simply 'About Love'. In the opening paragraphs of this story Alekhin philosophizes on love: 'we, when we love someone cannot stop asking ourselves questions: whether we are behaving honourably or dishonourably, sensibly or stupidly, what our love will lead to, and so forth. Whether this is a good thing or not I don't know, but one thing I do know—that all this is an interference, a pest, and it detracts from one's satisfaction.'

Alekhin illustrates his point by describing how his love for a married woman and hers for him is thwarted by their scruples with regard to her husband and family. Love, the story suggests, ought to be untrammelled by such considerations—should rise above petty human conventions. There is however no suggestion of rebellion against these conventions, but simply a thinly concealed yearning for the ideal world in which such an ideal love could flourish. 'The Lady with the Dog' conveys a similar feeling.

Love, as Alekhin sees it, is in fact almost divorced from human circumstances and reality. He refers to the case of a pretty servant-girl whose love for the brutish-looking cook seems inexplicable. Love, the implication is, is not an emotion to be implemented by man's reason, capable of being fitted by man into a scheme of things that would further his interests. This conception of love is commonplace enough; but Alekhin goes further. 'We do not know,' he says, 'how much questions of personal happiness matter in love.' It is no secret that love can lead to unhappiness, but Alekhin is saying that 'love' is of greater importance than the happiness it can bring: that it is, in fact, an end in itself. Nor is he talking of love for the divine—he is talking of love in the context of human relationships. What is the point of this love, it may be wondered, if questions of personal happiness do not come into account?

Chekhov himself would not perhaps have gone so far as to say this. When characters, even those whom he portrays sympathetically, start to 'talk philosophy', we may expect to hear extreme opinions which are not necessarily Chekhov's. Nevertheless, since in Chekhov's fiction the romantic heroine is overshadowed by the concept of an idealized love, the possibility springs to mind that Chekhov personally might have found this idealized love more alluring than the physical relationship or the 'human interest' that any specific liaison could offer him.

In the face of this possibility one of Chekhov's last stories leaps into significance. In December of 1897 Chekhov wrote 'A Visit to Friends' (*U znakomykh*). This story tells how one Podgorin is invited to spend a few days on the estate of Tatyana Loseva, an old acquaintance. He had as a student been in love with the younger sister, Nadezhda, although he had never actually proposed to her. Podgorin is still a bachelor: he has dealings with loose women on Malaya Bronnaya St. and other such parts of Moscow, but without any sense of involvement and even with some distaste. Nadezhda, or Nadya, who meets Podgorin at the station, at once suggests the romantic heroine: next to her brother-in-law, Tatyana's husband, she 'seemed ethereal': she is a pale-faced blonde of twenty-four, wearing a white dress with an open neck. But—and here is the surprise—Podgorin is displeased: 'her long bare white neck struck him as something new and not altogether agreeable': Nadya's behaviour strikes him as affected and unnatural. This is therefore no Misyus, the reader concludes: and indeed the climax of the story is in direct contrast to that of 'The Artist's Story'. It becomes apparent to Podgorin that he is expected to propose to Nadya. Walking in the garden one night, he realizes that Nadya is nearby, that she senses his presence and that 'white, pale, slim, very beautiful in the light of the moon, she was waiting to hear tender words'; but Podgorin 'felt irritated, and all he thought was that here on a country estate on a moonlit night, so close to a beautiful young girl dreaming of love, he was so unmoved that he might have been on Malaya Bronnaya St.—because, evidently, this sort of poetry had served its time for him, as had the other crude prose. Meetings on moonlit nights, white, slim-waisted figures and mysterious shadows ... had served their time ....'

Here then, in plain terms, we have a categorical rejection of the romantic heroines of Chekhov's earlier fiction—a rejection of both their physical trappings and of the aura of poetry which surrounds them.

The unexpectedness of such a statement demands some explanation. Podgorin, it might be alleged, is not necessarily Chekhov himself. But if Chekhov's apotheosis of a certain type of heroine and his poeticization of her has hitherto been, as it appears to have been, a strikingly idiosyncratic sentimentalization—idiosyncratic to the extent that it becomes monotonous to the reader who cannot share in the 'poetry'—it seems unlikely that Chekhov would shatter this private vision just for the sake of appearing unbiased. Podgorin is surely expressing something that Chekhov himself felt.

The critical point is that Podgorin is not averse to thinking about love; but only as something remote from the idea of a love-affair with Nadya, or indeed from any love-affair: 'he would have preferred ... some other woman, who standing ... where Nadya was standing now, would talk to him of something novel and interesting, having no relation to love or happiness, or, if she did talk of love, that it were a call to a new, wise and ennobling way of life, on the eve of which we are, perhaps, already living, and of which we sometimes have prescience.'

It is significant that Podgorin, as he walked in the garden, 'relapsed gradually into a mood of calm and peace; he felt that he was alone in the world and in the silence of the night the sound of his own footsteps seemed so sad.' But, melancholy though his sense of isolation may be, Podgorin does not welcome the sudden appearance of Nadya: on the contrary, he recoils from her. In the following chapters an attempt will be made to demonstrate that Podgorin's rejection of the romantic heroine is based on fear—on fear of intrusion into his solitude: and to suggest that in Chekhov also romance and the romantic heroine could inspire a similar fear.

NOTES

1. See, e.g., Shchepkina-Kupernik, p. 326, where she describes how not long before Chekhov's death Olga went off to the theatre with Nemirovich-Danchenko, telling her husband 'not to be bored and to be a good boy.' Chekhov then turned to Shchepkina-Kupernik and said: 'Yes ... it's time I was dead.' The anecdote is not intended to reflect well on Olga. See also: Nemirovich-Danchenko, *Chekhov*, p. 426, where he refers to Olga's jealousy of Chekhov's sister. This point was often made against Olga. See also: Rachmanowa, *passim*: Rachmanowa appears to be conducting a personal vendetta against Olga Knipper, in a tone which would invite a libel action from the latter had she still been alive.

2. Lykiardopoulos, reviewing *The Seagull* (p. 239), commented: 'The Moscow Art Theatre has today come to the conclusion that, even in Russia, a good Nina Zarechnaya is almost impossible to find.' How flat the play can fall if the audience cannot appreciate its symbolic atmosphere was demonstrated by its first-night failure on 17 October 1896.

EDMUND WILSON

Seeing Chekhov Plain

To write about Chekhov, for a critic of the English-speaking countries, has usually meant to grope among the incomplete and scrambled translations of Constance Garnett and others. Here is a book on the subject—*Chekhov: A Biographical and Critical Study*, by Ronald Hingley— by an Englishman who knows Russian and who has been able to avail himself of the new material published by the Soviets. It is a curious feature of Soviet life that the pitiless discouragement of talent in the field of contemporary literature has seemed hardly in the field of scholarship, to have affected the publication of editions of the Russian classics that are sometimes of unprecedented excellence. *The Complete Collected Works and Letters of A. P. Chekhov,* which was brought out in twenty volumes between 1944 and 1951, contains, in chronological sequence, every known piece of writing by Chekhov, published and unpublished, with all variants, early drafts, and passages suppressed by the censor. [I have since, however, learned from a paper by Gleb Struve that in the case of Chekhov's letters about the liquidated director Meyerhold, the Soviets have made suppressions of their own. 1971] At the time Mr. Hingley wrote his book, only the first eleven volumes had appeared, but with these, which included an immense amount of stuff that had been printed in magazines but that Chekhov had never collected—reviews and topical skits and captions for humorous drawings, and even a column of

From *A Window on Russia.* ©1972 by Farrar, Straus and Giroux, pp. 52-67. First published 1942. Reprinted by permission.

Moscow gossip that Chekhov contributed in his youth—Mr. Hingley
was in a better position to give an account of Chekhov's work than
anyone else, including Russians, who had even attempted to do so in
English. His book is clear, sensible, competent, and it should help to lift
the twilight atmosphere that has partly veiled Chekhov in English and
that is the result less, as people assume, of his moral and artistic qualities
than of the remoteness of Russia from us and of the obstacles between
us and his text.

For nothing could be more different from the Western conception
of Chekhov than that of the average literate Russian. In England and the
United States, Chekhov has been read almost exclusively by a specialized
literary public, with whom he has sometimes become a cult and by
whom he has been regarded as the master of so exquisite an art, so far
from obvious in its themes and technique, that one can only compare the
attitude toward him to the attitude toward Henry James at the time
when James had not yet come to figure as a pillar of the national
pantheon. But Chekhov's first publications were humorous sketches and
squibs contributed to magazines of the type of our old *Life* and *Puck*,
which he wrote, in his early twenties, in order to scrape together the
money to put himself through medical school, and among Russians he
has always had a public that, sometimes quite insensitive to his
masterpieces, never ceases to be delighted by the fantasy of this early
humor. The situation of Chekhov, in fact, from the point when he was
encouraged by the novelist Grigorovich, as Mark Twain was by Howells,
to take himself more seriously as a writer, was not unlike that of Mark
Twain when, after publishing *Huckleberry Finn*, he had difficulty in
sloughing off his original reputation as a popular entertainer. Some of
Chekhov's early comic stories—such as the one that appears in English
under the title *A Horsey Name*—have had much the same kind of success
as Mark Twain's *Jumping-Frog of Calaveras County*. They are so funny
that Chekhov the artist has had difficulty in living them down, though
the point of such a joke as *A Horsey Name* is involved with psychological
truth in a way that the Frog is not, and the element of humor in
Chekhov—though it certainly became more refined—has always been a
good deal stronger than non-Russian readers usually grasp.

The transition from the earlier to the later humor is well shown by
David Magarshack, a Russian-born Britisher who writes in English, in
another recent book on Chekhov, *Chekhov the Dramatist*. This transition

may be clearly traced in the successive revisions that have now been collected of the humorous dramatic monologue, *On the Harmfulness of Tobacco*, that eventually became and still remains a stock piece for recitation. The first version, of 1886, is a comic vaudeville turn full of touches from the barbershop weeklies, in which a lecturer against tobacco, who has turned up a little tipsy, loses the thread of his discourse, forgets himself sufficiently to produce a snuffbox, and confides in the audience at length on the subject of his shrewish wife and his many unmarriageable daughters—though even here it is the human situation that figures as the basis of the joke, and the lecturer's demoralization has already a touch of the macabre. The last version of this piece, written in 1902, at the end of Chekhov's life, is a horrifying and heartbreaking revelation of the pathetic personality of the lecturer: "Oh," he cries, in an outburst at the end, "to throw everything over! ... If only I could run away from this cheap and trashy and common life that's turning me into a pitiful old fool! ... Oh, to be able to get away somewhere, far far away in the fields, where I could stand like a tree, like a column, like a scarecrow in somebody's vegetable garden, underneath the wide sky, where you could watch the bright quiet moon hanging over you all the night, and forget, forget everything!" Then he catches sight of his slave-driving wife, who is watching him from the wings, and brings his lecture to a proper close. The different stages of this little play show in miniature Chekhov's whole growth.

Yet this humor that runs all through Chekhov is but one of a number of features that the foreigner may miss or misunderstand. If Chekhov has been baffling to Russians, it has been only because they wanted to pin him down to a definite political position, which he always refused to take. His work is not vague but compact and dense, all made up of hard detail and larded with allusions to specific things. Yet his stories as well as his plays, which have fascinated Western readers, have often left them puzzled or blank. To such readers—though, as much as those of Flaubert, as much as the plays of Ibsen or Shaw, these fictions are nailed to their time and place—they have seemed to occur in a realm of dream. "They are not lit [Chekhov's characters]," writes Mr. Somerset Maugham, in the preface to an omnibus of his own stories, "by the hard light of common day but suffused in a mysterious grayness. They move in this as though they were disembodied spirits. It is their souls that you seem to see. The subconscious seems to come to the surface and they communicate with one another directly, without the impediment of speech. Strange, futile creatures, with descriptions of their outward seeming tacked on them like a card on an exhibit in a museum, they move as mysteriously as the tortured souls who crowded about Dante when he walked in Hell. You have the feeling of a vast, gray, lost throng wandering aimless in some dim underworld." We can not, I think, however, entirely blame pale translations for the misty effect that Chekhov produces on Mr. Maugham. It is true that Constance Garnett made the Russian writers sound all more or less the same, whereas Chekhov's writing, though it sometimes lacks color, is never blurred in Russian; it gives rather the impression of the tight-strung lines of a masterly steel engraving. But, of course, Mr. Maugham is hardly at home in these questions of literary art. It is more interesting that Virginia Woolf should find herself at sea with Chekhov. "Our first impressions of Chekhov," she writes in *The Common Reader*, "are not of simplicity but of bewilderment. What is the point of it, and why does he make a story out of this? we ask as we read story after story.... These stories are inconclusive, we say, and proceed to frame a criticism based upon the assumption that stories ought to conclude in a way that we recognize.... We have to cast about in order to discover where the emphasis in these strange stories rightly comes.... Is it that he is primarily interested not in the soul's relation with other souls but with the soul's relation to health— with the soul's relation to goodness? These stories are always showing us some affectation, pose, insincerity. Some woman has got into a false relation; some man has been perverted by the inhumanity of his circumstances. The soul is ill; the soul is cured; the soul is not cured. Those are the emphatic points in his stories."

It is plain that to both these so different English novelists Chekhov comes as an apparition, rather insubstantial and eerie, abstracted from time and space, telling stories they can only half grasp. "I have little doubt," says Mr. Maugham, with a touch of that patronizing tone that he likes to adopt with his betters, "that Chekhov would have written stories with an ingenious, original, and striking plot if he had been able to think of them. It was not in his temperament. Like all good writers, he made a merit of his limitations." Well, Chekhov did contrive in his early phase—in the novel called in English *A Shooting Party* (Drama na Okhote)—a thriller that is certainly original and that is full of surprise and suspense. (It has recently been used for a Hollywood movie.) This novel, which was written as a job, as a serial for a magazine, is a highly characteristic work of astute social observation and shrewd psychological insight (it is strange to find Mr. Hingley describing this extraordinary story as "not of serious literary merit"); but Chekhov cared so little about plot-fiction that he never brought it out in a book. One cannot expect Mr. Maugham to approve of the precept that Ivan Bunin reports Chekhov's preaching to him: that in writing a short story you should lop off the beginning and the end. But it ought to be obvious to anyone whose notion of storytelling does not stop with the well-oiled plot, with the "wow" in the final paragraph which Chekhov refrained from writing, that the stories and plays of Chekhov are both complex and closely worked out. Mr. Hingley, who sometimes, in retelling Chekhov's stories, suggests that he has not seen their structure, does not bring out Chekhov's sense of form so well as Mr. Magarshack, who analyzes the patterns of the plays and demonstrates the subtlety and terseness of their beautiful workmanship. Yet there is no question that Western readers have been seriously handicapped with Chekhov even more than with the other Russian writers by their unfamiliarity with the cultural and social background of the world that he is writing about. He is much more limited and local than Tolstoy or Dostoevsky, and we do not always catch his allusions or understand the points he is trying to make. Though Chekhov is always specific, always quite sure and sharp, we think him elusive and vague. "These evocative undertones in the dialogue," Mr. Magarshack correctly writes of the literary references in Chekhov, "are completely lost in the translation, with the result that an English version of a Chekhov play distorts the emotional reaction it is meant to set up in the audience, creating the impression that the characters express themselves so oddly because they are 'Russians.'" Nor are the full social implications of Chekhov's characters grasped. In the case of Mrs. Woolf, for example, she has touched upon something essential in Chekhov, something that can be understood anywhere, and if Chekhov had no general human significance, he would not belong to the great Russian tradition and would never, outside of Russia, have exerted so strong an influence. Yet it is also in the Russian tradition to deal critically with Russia's specific problems, and Chekhov was no exception to this. He did not have a religious message, as Dostoevsky and Tolstoy did, and he deliberately kept clear of politics, but, after all, his story *Ward No. 6* was one of the contemporary writings that most aroused Lenin in his youth, and his whole work is a social document of a powerful if largely negative kind.

A further and unnecessary obstacle to the foreigner's under-standing of Chekhov has been added by the Garnett translation, which jumbles the stories up, giving no indication of when they were written and sometimes putting side by side productions divided by decades, in such a way as to destroy completely the sequence of some twenty-five years of work. D. S. Mirsky complained of this in his *Contemporary Russian Literature*, and Mr. Hingley makes the point again. In the Russian editions the stories are usually presented in their proper order, and in the new Soviet edition each has been carefully dated. It is only by reading them thus that it is possible to get any idea of Chekhov's artistic development or his ultimate vision of Russian life.

If we follow this line of development, we see that, beginning with satirical jokes, Chekhov goes on to master the art of the ironic anecdote, so often pathetic or tragic (it would hardly, one would think, be possible to complain of a good many of them that one did not understand the point); these, in turn, begin to expand into something more rounded-out (the dense but concise study of character and situation) and eventually—in what Mr. Hingley calls Chekhov's Tolstoyan period (*A Nervous Breakdown*, for example)—take on a new moral interest or attain, as in his "clinical" one (*The Black Monk*), a new psychological depth. These studies become more comprehensive—*The Steppe, A Dreary Story, Ward No. 6*—in such a way as to cover a whole life *en raccourci* or an experience in fuller detail. Such pieces are not short stories but what Henry James called *nouvelles*. (The earlier *Shooting Party* was Chekhov's only real novel.) Then Chekhov enters his final phase, which extends from 1894 to his death in 1904, and which it seems to me possible to date from the story called *A Woman's Kingdom*, which immediately follows *The Black Monk*. The *Monk* had been a masterpiece of a kind different from any of these later ones: a story of the supernatural that had something in common with Hawthorne, though it was also a "clinical" story of a psychiatric case; and all through the stories before this, even when they were dealing with lives that were sordid or uneventful, there had run a certain vein of the grotesque, of something not always quite plausible: an element of satiric relief of comic exaggeration—even, in certain cases, of fable and fairy tale. But there is nothing of this in *A Woman's Kingdom*, which simply describes a day in the household of an unmarried woman—

a chronicle of domestic incident, solidly and soberly treated, in which the rise of the industrial middle class (the theme of a number of the later stories) is given its first intensive treatment. The method here changes as well as the scale. We now rarely get a single situation—as in *Ward No. 6*—carried through to an ironic climax.

This final series of stories, of which Chekhov managed to produce only a few a year, become more and more complex, involving a number of characters and presenting, as his plays of these years do, a whole social microcosm. These are really compressed novels, and we soon come to see that Chekhov is composing, in this latest period, a kind of Comédie Humaine in miniature. He is covering contemporary Russia in a sequence of significant studies, each one or each group of which aims to deal with—and for the purposes of the author more or less to exhaust—some clearly defined milieu. He is certainly concentrating here on an anatomy of Russian society rather than on appraising the soundness, as Virginia Woolf found him doing, of this or that individual soul. In *A Woman's Kingdom* (Babye Tsarstvo), and later on in *A Doctor's Visit* (Sluchay iz Praktiki) and *The New Villa*, it is the recently arrived *bourgeoisie*, who have grown up with modern factories and modern engineering and now find themselves cut off from the people, from whom they have sprung. In *Three Years*, it is the old Moscow merchant world, almost as self-contained as a ghetto, in which the strength of the older generation, bigoted, harsh, and oppressive, is at last undermined by the defection of its sons, who are marrying into the gentry or attempting, as intelligentsia, to escape to a world of more freedom and more sophistication; but these latter do not pan out, they cannot adapt themselves, and the wife of the brother who has stayed with the business—a woman from a "county" family, who has suffered a good deal from her boorish in-laws—comes to feel in the long run that her husband has chosen the better part. In *The Murder*, it is a family of innkeepers who have learned to read the Bible and are possessed by fanatical religious ideas—a form of illumination that does not save them from benighted savagery. *Peasants* is a study of the peasant world, which Chekhov is far from idealizing, as Tolstoy liked to do, or sentimentalizing, as Turgenev sometimes did. A peasant from the *izba*, who has bettered himself to the extent of becoming a waiter in Moscow, falls ill and returns with a wife and child to his family in the village; here, surrounded by miseries and horrors to which he has become unaccustomed, he is allowed to die of tuberculosis, while his wife and his daughter sink to the sordid and servile level of the older generation. In a companion piece, *In the Ravine*, Chekhov deals with the brutalizing influence of the kulak, prosperous peasant, class. In this somewhat better-off family, the shopkeeper father sells bad meat, one of his sons passes bad money, and an enterprising daughter-in-law, who is building a brickyard on her father-in-law's land and who fears that she may be deprived of it, eliminates the infant grandson to whom he proposes to leave it by scalding him to death with boiling water. Everybody knows about this but the poorer peasants do not dare protest, and nothing is done about it. These two stories of peasant life are like cultures of malignant germs examined through a microscope. In *The Bishop*, the next-to-last story that Chekhov lived to complete, he fixes on his slide a specimen of the not quite diseased yet not very vigorous tissue of the Greek Orthodox Church: a dying peasant priest, who has risen above the level of his parents but now finds he has nobody close to him; who has been turned into a professional churchman, caught up in the routine of his duties, without ever having experienced a moment of genuine religious feeling; who should clearly have been a lay intellectual but has never had the chance of becoming one. In these, and in the stories that immediately precede them, are presented a variety of other types of peasants, ex-peasants, and the lower middle class that were called in Russian *meshchane*, together with doctors, professors, petty provincial officials, and—given the full-scale treatment in *The Duel* of 1891—the pretentious and inept intelligentsia.

It should be noted that in his stories of this period Chekhov gives us no comparable picture of the decaying landowner class that is the subject of three of his later plays, and that this class, when it does appear—the story called in English *An Artist's Story* is the only possible exception—figures usually, as in *My Life*, in only an incidental role and is shown as degenerate to the point of squalor. There are here no lakes with symbolic gulls, no cherry orchards in bloom. Mr. Magarshack makes a great point of Chekhov's repeated insistence that *The Cherry Orchard* was meant as a comedy not far removed from farce, declaring that the author's intention was betrayed by Stanislavsky when he turned it into something romantic, and it is true that if one reads the play, one finds that the humor is broader, the glamour laid on less thick, than memories of the Art Theater productions, seen without one's knowing the language, might have led one to expect. Yet the poetry and pathos *are* there—Chekhov put them there. Mr. Magarshack is certainly mistaken when he thinks that it was not Chekhov's purpose to have us think that the old butler Firs is to die in the boarded-up house, abandoned by his irresponsible masters. My own explanation of Chekhov's complaints about Stanislavsky's production of *The Cherry Orchard* is that he felt himself somewhat embarrassed by his tenderness, in these later plays, for the world of the *dvoryane*, the gentry, into which he had not been born and toward which he had otherwise taken a rather disdainful tone. If he seems to protest too much in his letters on the subject of *The Cherry Orchard*, we may guess that he wished to avoid being thought to admire it too much (as Dickens, in *Our Mutual Friend*, disturbed by the threatening power of the parvenu middle class, was moved to a certain nostalgia for the cultivated upper classes he had hitherto ignored or made fun of). Yet Lopakhin, who buys up the cherry orchard—a freed serf, like Chekhov's father—but who cannot, on account of his origins, induce even a poor relation of the original owners to marry him, is hardly more of a hero to Chekhov than the narrator of *A Shooting Party*. This narrator, a clever but common man, a provincial examining magistrate, both despises and envies the local count, proprietor of a run-down estate and a degenerating household not unlike but very much less attractive than those of *The Cherry Orchard*, and murders with impunity, under the nobleman's nose, a girl who has been the mistress of both of them when she shows that she prefers the count, however unappetizing, to the narrator, for whom she feels some physical passion. He completely bluffs the district authorities and succeeds in getting an innocent peasant sent away to Siberia for the crime he himself has committed, and eventually takes the count in to live with him, when the latter has drunk away all his money, still susceptible to the old man's prestige and in consequence enjoying his degradation. This lower-class man who is on the make is the central figure in Chekhov. This is the theme—transposed into terms of a variety of milieux—of every one of the stories mentioned above. And it is much to the point at the present time to inquire how Chekhov judged these characters. For it was people of this kind who came to the top with the success of the Russian Revolution. It is an irony in Chekhov's own manner that, in carefully preserving his work, the Soviet Russians should always assume—when they talk about him in public, at any rate—that his types are all monsters and parasites produced by the corruption of the old regime, when, in their groveling before authority, their half-baked education and their vulgar ambitions, they have obviously a good deal in common with the people who are running the Soviet Union.

What, then, did Chekhov think of these people, of whom he had been one himself and from whose cowardices, servilities, hypocrisies he prided himself—in a remarkable letter quoted by Mr. Hingley—on having delivered himself, declaring that he had succeeded in finally "squeezing out of myself every drop of servile blood" and becoming "a real human being." He seemed to be well aware that the future belongs to them. Mr. Hingley devotes some space to discussing the unreal problem of whether Chekhov ought to be regarded as an "optimistic" or a "pessimistic" writer. "There is," he says, "general agreement in Russia today that Chekhov was an optimist, both in his writings and in his personal life, and this view has the important support of Chekhov himself." Mr. Magarshack insists that Chekhov's last four plays represent "a drama of courage and hope." Now, it is true that an occasional speech in these plays gives expression to courage or hope, but when any such note is struck—as it is at the end of *The Three Sisters*, when the husbandless, loverless women, unable to make a break with the life of their backwater town, begin to talk of a time when "our sufferings will pass into joy for those who live after us" and "peace and happiness will reign on earth"—such longings and resolutions are always seen in a pathetic perspective. It is true that Chekhov himself was occasionally moved to prophesy in a similar sense. "Do you know," A. A. Kuprin reports him as saying, "in three or four hundred years the whole earth will turn into a blossoming garden." But the immediate prospect for a world administered by Chekhov's characters is not in the least cheerful. One cannot, of course, expect a robust faith from a man who is dying of tuberculosis, though such invalids have their moments of buoyancy, but Chekhov's susceptibility to this disease—from which a number of his later characters, such as Nikolai in *Peasants*, suffer—was itself no doubt partly a product of the hard strain of adaptation, intellectual, social and physical, that so many of his characters undergo. "What the writers who belong to the gentry," he wrote in a latter of 1889, "receive as a gift from nature we lower-class intelligentsia buy at the cost of our youth," and this cost in debilitating effort and the frequent inadequacy of what it bought were usually in the foreground with Chekhov. Yet, in one of his best stories, *The Steppe*, he makes us feel that the hopes of the peasants who are sending their boy away to be educated may be something more than merely touching, that something new and sound may come of it—though the bishop of the next-to-last story might well be this boy grown old, who, cut off from his peasant mother, has never found his true vocation.

But—what is curious and probably significant, as it is certainly rather surprising to the reader who has taken these pieces in their chronological order—the last story that Chekhov completed, *Betrothed* (Nevesta) (buried by Mrs. Garnett in a volume of pieces of much earlier date), sounds a note of triumphant self-confidence. A girl from the provinces, an independent spirit, throws over her provincial fiancé, whose *posh-lost*, that special combination of commonness, banality and smugness, she finds that she cannot stomach. She has been worked on by an artist cousin, who has told her that she must go to St. Petersburg and study in the university, that the more people like her become "dedicated" and trained, "the sooner the Kingdom of Heaven will descend upon the earth. In that time, little by little, there will not be left of your town one stone upon another. Everything will be turned upside down; everything will be changed, as if by magic. There will arise large and splendid houses, marvellous parks, extraordinary fountains, remarkable people." This cousin, a typical Chekhovian *raté*, has slipped out of painting into architecture, out of architecture into working for a lithographer, and has never been effectual at anything except egging on his women friends to throw over their family life. Unlike the three sisters, the Nadya of this story does succeed in making the break, and she finds, when she returns for vacation, that her home now seems small and ignoble. She is repelled by the ancient tradition, carried on by her mother and grandmother, of crowding all the servants into narrow quarters and making them sleep on the floor. She does not feel very much compunction at discovering that this mother and grandmother have been dropped by their social circle as the result of her improper behavior in jilting her fiancé. She is not very much moved at receiving a telegram which tells her that the cousin who spurred her on has died of tuberculosis. She shakes off the old house and town—it is as if the old life had burned up and the ashes had blown away—and, alive with excitement and hope, she goes back to her work in the city.

Chekhov, thus, at the end of his life, reminds us of the Watcher by the Way in that fine poem of Edwin Arlington Robinson's, *The Town Down the River*. Robinson was dealing here, within only a few years of Chekhov, with a period in the United States that seemed sometimes, though not for quite the same reasons, as discouraging, as full of frustrations, as the Russia of his time did to Chekhov. Robinson's watcher by the road that leads to a great modern city warns the people who are eagerly journeying there, as the characters of Chekhov do to Moscow and St. Petersburg, of its dangers and disillusions. Yet when his own life is nearly over, and the old and unsuccessful come to him to tell him that they now see he was right and to warn him in turn that his end is near and that they might as well all give up their hopes:

> "But your lanterns are unlighted
> And the Town is far before you:
> Let us hasten, I implore you,"
> Said the Watcher by the Way.
> "Long have I waited,
> Longer have I known
> That the Town would have its own,
> And the call be for the fated.
>
> "In the name of all created,
> Let us hear no more, my brothers;
> Are we older than all others?
> Are the planets in our way?"
> "Hark," said one; "I hear the River,
> Calling always, night and day."
> "Forward, then! The lights are shining,"
> Said the Watcher by the Way.

November 22, 1952

D. S. MIRSKY

Chekhov*

Anton Pavlovich Chekhov (1860–1904) was born at Taganrog, on the sea of Azov. His grandfather had been a serf ... but had acquired considerable wealth by trade and was able to purchase his freedom and that of all his family. Chekhov's parents were simple, half-educated, very religious people, with a strong family feeling. The family consisted of several sons and a daughter. They were all given a liberal education. Anton, who was the youngest but one, was sent to the gymnasium (secondary school) of Taganrog. But while he was there the prosperity of the Chekhovs came to an end. The building of a railway through the neighboring Rostov was a severe blow to the commerce of Taganrog, and Paul Chekhov soon saw himself forced to close his business. In 1876 he left Taganrog and went to seek employment in Moscow. Anton remained alone in Taganrog. In 1879 he finished his time at the gymnasium and went to Moscow to join his family. He was matriculated as a student of the Faculty of Medicine. After the normal course of five years, he took his degree in 1884. From his arrival in Moscow to his death he never parted from his parents and sister, and as his literary income soon became important, he early became the mainstay of his family. The Chekhovs were an exceptionally united family—a case exceedingly rare among the intelligentsia, and owing, of course, to their peasant and merchant origins.

From *A History of Russian Literature*, as reprinted in *Anton Chekhov's Short Stories*, ed. Ralph Matlaw. © 1979, W.W. Norton, pp. 291-301. Reprinted by permission.

Chekhov began working in the comic papers the year he came to Moscow, and before he left the university he had become one of their most welcome contributors. So on taking his degree, he did not settle down to practice as a doctor, but fell back on his literary work for subsistence. In 1886 some of his comic stories were collected in book form. The book had an immediate success with the public and was soon followed by another volume of comic stories. The critics, especially the radical critics, took little notice of the book, but it attracted the attention of two influential men of letters—the veteran novelist Grigorovich and Suvorin, editor of the pro-government *New Times*, the largest daily paper of the day. The shrewd and clever Suvorin at once saw the great possibilities of Chekhov and invited him to contribute to his paper, where he even started a special weekly literary supplement for Chekhov. They became close friends, and in Chekhov's correspondence his letters to Suvorin form undoubtedly the most interesting part. Chekhov had now gained a firm footing in "big literature" and was free from the tyranny of the comic papers. This change in his social position was followed by a change in his work—he abandoned comic writing and developed the style that is most characteristically his. This change is apparent in the stories written by him in 1886–7. At the same time Chekhov wrote his first play, *Ivanov*, which was produced in Moscow in December 1887 and in Petersburg a year later. It is characteristic of this period of transition that Chekhov continued working at these pieces after their first publication; *The Steppe* and *Ivanov* that are now reproduced in his *Works* are very different from what first appeared in 1887. Henceforward Chekhov's life was rather uneventful, and what events there were, are closely connected with his writings. An isolated episode was his journey to Sakhalin, the Russian Botany Bay. He went there in 1890, traveling through Siberia (before the days of the Trans-Siberian) and returning by sea via Ceylon. He made a very thorough investigation of convict life and published the result of it in a separate book (*Sakhalin Island*, 1891). It is remarkable for its thoroughness, objectivity, and impartiality, and is an important historical document. It is supposed to have influenced certain reforms in prison life introduced in 1892. This journey was Chekhov's greatest practical contribution to the humanitarianism that was so near to his heart. In private life he was also very kindhearted and generous. He gave away much of his money.

His native town of Taganrog was the recipient of a library and a museum from him.

In 1891 Chekhov was rich enough to buy a piece of land at Melikhovo, some fifty miles south of Moscow. There he settled down with his parents, sister, and younger brother, and lived for six years. He took part in local life and spent much money on local improvements. In 1892–3, during the cholera epidemic, he worked as the head of a sanitary district. Here it was he wrote many of his best and most mature stories. He remained at Melikhovo till 1897, when the state of his health forced him to move. Consumption had set in, and he had to spend the rest of his life mainly between the south coast of the Crimea and foreign— French and German—health resorts. This was not the only change in his life. All his surroundings changed, owing to his new connection with the Moscow Art Theater and his more decided political orientation towards the left. This latter led to his breach with Suvorin, to whom he wrote a very angry letter in connection with the Dreyfus affair (even in Russia the *Affaire* was a hotbed of quarrel!) and to his friendship with the younger generation of writers, headed by Gorky and distinctly revolutionary. During these last years (especially after 1900, when he settled down in Yalta) he saw much of Tolstoy. In the popular opinion of that time, Chekhov, Gorky, and Tolstoy formed a sort of sacred trinity symbolizing all that was best in independent Russia as opposed to the dark forces of Tsarism. Chekhov lived up to his liberal reputation, and when the Academy, following a hint of the government, excluded Gorky from its membership almost immediately after electing him, Chekhov, like the veteran socialist Korolenko, resigned his membership. But from the literary point of view this phase is hardly of much importance—it introduced no new elements into his work. Far more important is his connection with the Art Theater. After *Ivanov*, Chekhov had written several light one-act comedies that had a considerable success with the public but added little to his intrinsic achievement. In 1895 he turned once more to serious drama and wrote *The Seagull* (as it is called in the English translation, rather absurdly—the Russian *Chayka* means just *Gull*). It was produced at the State Theater of Petersburg in 1896. It was badly understood by the actors and badly acted. The first night was a smashing failure. The play was hissed down, and the author, confounded by his defeat, left the theater after the second act and escaped to Melikhovo, vowing never again to write a play. Meanwhile K. S.

Stanislavsky (Alekseyev), a wealthy merchant of Moscow, and the dramatist Vladimir Nemirovich-Danchenko founded the Art Theater, which was to be such an important landmark in the history of the Russian stage. They succeeded in getting *The Seagull* for one of their first productions. The cast worked at it with energy and understanding, and when the play was acted by them in 1898, it proved a triumphant success. Chekhov turned with new energy towards dramatic writing, and wrote his most famous plays with a direct view to Stanislavsky's casts. *Uncle Vanya* (which had been planned as early as 1888) was produced in 1900, *The Three Sisters* in 1901, and *The Cherry Orchard* in January 1904. Each play was a greater triumph than the preceding one. There was complete harmony among playwright, actors, and public. Chekhov's fame was at its height. However, he did not become so rich as to compare with Kipling, or D'Annunzio, or even with Gorky. For like his favorite heroes, he was eminently unpractical: in 1899 he sold all the works he had hitherto written to the publisher Marx for 75,000 rubles ($37,500). It turned out after the transaction that Marx was not aware of the extent of his writings—he had reckoned on four volumes of short stories, and he had unconsciously bought nine! In 1901 Chekhov married an actress of the Art Theater, Olga L. Knipper; so his life became further changed. These last years he lived mostly at Yalta, where he had built a villa. He was constantly besieged by importunate admirers, with whom he was very patient and kind. In June 1904 his illness had so advanced that he was sent by the doctors to Badenweiler, a small health resort in the Black Forest, where he died. His body was brought to Moscow and buried by the side of his father, who had preceded him in 1899.

Chekhov's literary career falls into two distinct periods: before and after 1886.[1] The English reader and the more "literary" Russian public know him by his later work, but it may be safely asserted that a much greater number of Russians know him rather as the author of his early comic stories than as the author of *My Life* and *Three Sisters*. It is a characteristic fact that many of his most popular and typical comic stories, precisely those which are sure to be known to every middle-class or semi-educated Russian (for example, *A Horse Name*, *Vint*, *The Complaint Ledger*, *Surgery*), were not translated into English. It is true that some of these stories are very difficult to translate, so topical and national are the jokes. But it is also evident that the English-speaking admirer of Chekhov has no taste for this buffoonery but looks to Chekhov for commodities of a very different description. The level of the comic papers in which Chekhov wrote was by no means a high one. They were a sanctuary of every kind of vulgarity and bad taste. Their buffoonery was vulgar and meaningless. They lacked the noble gift of nonsense, which of all things elevates man nearest the gods; they lacked wit, restraint, and grace. It was mere trivial buffoonery and Chekhov's stories stand in no striking contrast to their general background. Except for a higher degree of craftsmanship, they are of a piece with the rest. Their dominant note is an uninspired sneer at the weaknesses and follies of mankind, and it would need a more than lynx-eyed critic to discern in them the note of human sympathy and of the higher humor that is so familiar to the reader of Chekhov's mature work. The great majority of these stories were never reprinted by Chekhov, but still the first and second volumes of his collected edition contain several dozen of the kind. Only a few—and all of them of a less crude variety—have had the honor of an English translation. But even in the crudest, Chekhov stands out as a superior craftsman, and in the economy of his means there is a promise of *Sleepy* and *At Christmas-time*. Before long, Chekhov began to deviate from the straight line imposed on him by the comic papers, and as early as 1886 he could write such a story as *The Chorus Girl*, which may yet be a little primitive and clumsy in its lyrical construction but on the whole stands almost on a level with the best of his mature work. *Parti-colored Stories*, which appeared in 1886 and laid the foundation of Chekhov's reputation in the literary circles, contained, besides many exercises in crude buffoonery, stories of a different kind that presented a gay appearance but were sad in substance—and that answered admirably to the hackneyed phrase of Russian critics, "tears through laughter." Such, for instance, is *Misery*: on a wet winter night a cabman who has just lost his son tries to tell his story to one after another of his fares and does not succeed in kindling their sympathy.

In 1886, as had been said, Chekhov was able to free himself from the comic papers and could now develop a new style that had begun to assert itself somewhat earlier. This style was (and remained) essentially poetical, but it was some time before he finally settled the main lines of what was to be the characteristic Chekhovian story. In his stories of 1886–8 there are many elements that have been yet imperfectly blended—a strain of descriptive journalism (in its most unadulterated form in *Uprooted*); pure anecdote, sometimes just ironical (*The First-Class Passenger*), sometimes poignantly tragicomical (*Vanka*); the lyrical expression of atmosphere (*The Steppe, Happiness*); psychological studies of morbid experience (*Typhus*); parables and moralities laid out in a conventional, un-Russian surrounding (*The Bet, A Story without a Title*). But already one of the favorite and most characteristic themes asserts its domination—the mutual lack of understanding between human beings, the impossibility for one person to feel in tune with another. *The Privy Councilor, The Post, The Name-Day Party, The Princess*, are all based on this idea—which becomes something like the leitmotiv of all Chekhov's later work. The most typical stories of this period are all located in the country of his early life, the steppe between the Sea of Azov and the Donets. These are *The Steppe, Happiness, The Horse-Stealers*. They are planned as lyrical symphonies (though the last one is also an anecdote). Their dominant note is superstition, the vague terror (Chekhov makes it poetical) before the presences that haunt the dark and empty steppe, the profound uninterestingness and poverty of the steppe peasant's life, a vague hope of a happiness that may be discovered, with the help of dark powers, in some ancient treasure mound. *The Steppe*, at which Chekhov worked much and to which he returned again after its publication, is the central thing in this period. It lacks the wonderful architecture of his short stories—it is a lyrical poem, but a poem made out of the substance of trivial, dull, and dusky life. The long, monotonous, uneventful journey of a little boy over the endless steppe from his native village to a distant town is drawn out in a hundred pages to form a languid, melodious, and tedious lullaby. A brighter aspect of Chekhov's lyrical art is in *Easter Eve*. The monk on night duty on the ferryboat tells a passenger about his dead fellow monk, who had the rare gift of writing lauds to the saints. He describes with loving detail the technique of this art, and one discerns Chekhov's sincere sympathy for this unnoticed, unwanted, quiet, and unambitious fellow craftsman. To the same period belongs *Kashtanka*, the delightful history of a dog that was kidnaped by a circus clown to form part of a troupe of performing animals and escaped to her old master in the middle of a performance. The story is a wonderful blend of humor and poetry, and though it certainly sentimentalizes and humanizes its animals, one cannot help recognizing it as a masterpiece. Another little gem is *Sleepy*, a real masterpiece of concentration, economy, and powerful effectiveness.[2]

In some stories of this period we find already the manner that is pre-eminently Chekhovian. The earliest story where it is quite distinctly discernible is *The Name-Day Party* (1887), on which Chekhov himself laid a great value, but which is not yet perfect; he confesses in a letter to Suvorin that he "would gladly have spent six months over *The Name-Day Party*.... But what am I to do? I begin a story on September 10th with the thought that I must finish it by October 5th at the latest; if I don't, I shall fail the editor and be left without money. I let myself go at the beginning and write with an easy mind; but by the time I get to the middle, I begin to grow timid and fear that my story will be too long.... This is why the beginning of my stories is always very promising ... the middle is huddled and timid, and the end is, as in a short sketch, like fireworks."[3] But the essential of Chekhov's mature style is unmistakably present. It is the "biography" of a mood developing under the trivial pinpricks of life, but owing in substance to a deep-lying, physiological or psychological cause (in this case the woman's pregnancy). *A Dreary Story*, published in 1889, may be considered the starting point of the mature period. The leitmotiv of mutual isolation is brought out with great power. We may date the meaning that has come to be associated in Russia with the words "Chekhovian state of mind" (*Chekhovskoye nastroyenie*) from *A Dreary Story*. The atmosphere of the story is produced by the professor's deep and growing disillusionment as to himself and the life around him, the gradual loss of faith in his vocation, the gradual drifting apart of people linked together by life. The professor realizes the meaninglessness of his life—and the "giftlessness" (*bezdarnost*, a characteristically Chekhovian word) and dullness of all that surrounds him. His only remaining friend, his former ward Katya, an unsuccessful disillusioned actress, breaks down under an intenser experience of the same feelings. And though his affection for her is sincere and genuine, and though he is suffering from the same causes as she is, he fails to find the necessary language to approach her. An unconquerable inhibition keeps him closed to her, and all he can say to her is:

> "Let us have lunch, Katya."
> "No, thank you," she answers coldly.
> Another minute passes in silence.
> "I don't like Kharkov," I say; "it is so gray here—such a gray town."

"Yes, perhaps.... It's ugly.... I am here not for long, passing through. I am going on to-day."

"Where?"

"To the Crimea ... that is, to the Caucasus."

"Oh! For long?"

"I don't know."

"Katya gets up and, with a cold smile, holds out her hand, looking at me. I want to ask her: 'Then you won't be at my funeral?' but she does not look at me; her hand is cold and, as it were, strange. I escort her to the door in silence. She goes out, walks down the long corridor, without looking back. She knows that I am looking after her, and she will look back at the turn. No, she did not look round. I've seen her black dress for the last time; her steps have died away! ... Farewell, my treasure!"[4]

This ending on a minor note is repeated in all Chekhov's subsequent stories and gives the keynote to his work.

A Dreary Story opens the succession of Chekhov's mature masterpieces. Besides the natural growth of his genius, he was now free to work longer over them than he could when he was writing *The Name-Day Party*. So his stories written in the nineties are almost without exception perfect works of art. It is mainly on the work of this period that Chekhov's reputation now rests. The principal stories written after 1889 are, in chronological order, *The Duel, Ward No. 6* (1892), *An Anonymous Story* (1893), *The Black Monk, The Teacher of Literature* (1894), *Three Years, Ariadne, Anna on the Neck, The House with the Mansard, My Life* (1895), *Peasants* (1897), *The Darling, Ionych, The Lady with the Dog* (1898), *The New Villa* (1899), *At Christmas-time, In the Ravine* (1900). After this date (it was the period of *Three Sisters* and *The Cherry Orchard*) he wrote only two stories, *The Bishop* (1902) and *Betrothed* (1903).

Chekhov's art has been called Psychological, but it is psychological in a very different sense from Tolstoy's, Dostoyevsky's, or Marcel Proust's. No writer excels him in conveying the mutual unsurpassable isolation of human beings and the impossibility of understanding each other. This idea forms the core of almost every one of his stories, but, in spite of this, Chekhov's characters are singularly lacking in individual personality. Personality is absent from his stories. His characters all speak (within class limits and apart from the little tricks of catchwords he lends them from time to time) the same language, which is Chekhov's own. They cannot be recognized, as Tolstoy's and Dostoyevsky's can, by the mere *sound of their voices*. They are all alike, all made of the same material—"the common stuff of humanity"—and in this sense Chekhov is the most "democratic," the most "unanimist," of all writers. For of course the similarity of all his men and women is not a sign of weakness—it is the expression of his fundamental intuition of life as a homogeneous matter but cut out into water-tight compartments by the phenomenon of individuality. Like Stendhal and the French classicists, and unlike Tolstoy, Dostoyevsky, and Proust, Chekhov is a student of "man in general." But unlike the classicists, and like Proust, he fixes his attention on the infinitesimals, the "pinpricks" and "straws" of the soul. Stendhal deals in psychological "whole numbers." He traces the major, conscious, creative lines of psychical life. Chekhov concentrates on the "differentials" of mind, its minor, unconscious, involuntary, destructive, and dissolvent forces. As art, Chekhov's method is active—more active than, for instance, Proust's, for it is based on a stricter and a more conscious *choice* of material and a more complicated and elaborate disposition of it. But as "outlook," as "philosophy," it is profoundly passive and "nonresistant," for it is a surrender to the "micro-organisms," of the soul, to its destructive microbes. Hence the general impressions produced by the whole of Chekhov's work that he had a cult for inefficiency and weakness. For Chekhov has no other way of displaying his sympathy with his characters than to show in detail the process of their submission to their microbes. The strong man who does not succumb in this struggle, or who does not experience it, is always treated by Chekhov with less sympathy and comes out as the "villain of the play"—in so far as the word "villain" is at all applicable to the world Chekhov moves in. The strong man in this world of his is merely the insensate brute, with a skin thick enough not to feel the "pinpricks," which are the only important thing in life. Chekhov's art is constructive. But the construction he uses is not a narrative construction—it might rather be called musical; not, however, in the sense that his prose is melodious, for it is not. But his method of constructing a story is akin to the method used in music. His stories are at once fluid and precise. The lines along which he builds them are very complicated curves, but they have been calculated with the utmost precision. A story by him is a series of points marking out with precision the lines discerned by him in the tangled web of consciousness. Chekhov excels in the art of tracing the first stages of an emotional process; in indicating those first symptoms of a deviation when to the general eye, and to the conscious eye of the subject in question, the nascent curve still seems to coincide with a straight line. An infinitesimal touch, which at first hardly arrests the reader's attention, gives a hint at the direction the story is going to take. It is then repeated as a leitmotiv, and at each repetition the true equation of the curve becomes more apparent, and it ends by shooting away in a direction very different from that of the original straight line. Such stories as *The Teacher of Literature*, *Ionych*, and *The Lady with the Dog* are perfect examples of such emotional curves. The straight line, for instance, in *Ionych* is the doctor's love for Mlle Turkin; the curve, his subsidence into the egoistical complacency of a successful provincial career. In *The Teacher of Literature* the straight line is again the hero's love; the curve, his dormant dissatisfaction with selfish happiness and his intellectual ambition. In *The Lady with the Dog* the straight line is the hero's attitude towards his affair with the lady as a trivial and passing intrigue; the curve, his overwhelming and all-pervading love for her. In most of Chekhov's stories these constructive lines are complicated by a rich and mellow atmosphere, which he produces by the abundance of emotionally significant detail. The effect is poetical, even lyrical: as in a lyric, it is not interest in the development that the reader feels, but "infection" by the poet's mood. Chekhov's stories are lyrical monoliths; they cannot be dissected into episodes, for every episode is strictly conditioned by the whole and is without significance apart from it. In architectural unity Chekhov surpasses all Russian writers of the realistic age. Only in Pushkin and Lermontov do we find an equal or superior gift of design. Chekhov thought Lermontov's *Taman* was the best short story ever written, and this partiality was well founded. *Taman* forestalled Chekhov's method of lyrical construction. Only its air is colder and clearer than the mild and mellow "autumnal" atmosphere of Chekhov's world.

Two of his best stories, *My Life* and *In the Ravine*, stand somewhat apart from the rest of his mature work. *My Life* is the story of a Tolstoyan, and one cannot help thinking that in it Chekhov tried to approach the clearer and more intellectual style of Tolstoy. There are a directness of narrative and a thinness of atmosphere that are otherwise rare in Chekhov. In spite of this relative absence of atmosphere, it is perhaps his most poetically pregnant story. It is convincingly symbolical. The hero, his father, his sister, the Azhogins, and Anyuta Blagovo stand out with the distinctness of morality characters. The very vagueness and generality of its title helps to make it something like an *Everyman*. For poetical grasp and significance *My Life* may be recognized as the masterpiece of Chekhov—unless it is surpassed by *In the Ravine*. This, one of his last stories, is an amazing piece of work. The scene is the Moscow Industrial area—it is the history of a shopkeeper's family. It is remarkably free from all excess of detail, and the atmosphere is produced, with the help of only a few descriptive touches, by the movement of the story. It is infinitely rich in emotional and symbolical significance. What is rare in Chekhov—in both these stories there is an earnestness, a keenness of moral judgment that raises them above the average of his work. All Chekhov's work is symbolical, but in most of his stories the symbolism is less concrete and more vaguely suggestive. It is akin to Maeterlinck's, in spite of the vast difference of style between the Russian realist and the Belgian mystic. *Ward No. 6*, the darkest and most terrible of all Chekhov's stories, is an especially notable example of this suggestive symbolism. It is all the more suggestive for being strictly realistic. (The only time Chekhov attempted to step out of the limits of strict realism was when he wrote the only story that is quite certainly a failure—*The Black Monk*.) But this symbolism reached its full development in his plays, beginning with *The Seagull*.

* * *

Chekhov's English admirers think that everything is perfect in Chekhov. To find weak spots in him will seem blasphemy to them. Still it is only fair to point out these spots. I have already referred to the complete lack of individuality in his characters and in their way of speaking. This is not in itself a fault, for it belongs to his fundamental intuition of life, which recognizes no personality. But it is not a virtue. It is especially noticeable when he makes his characters speak at length on abstract subjects. How different from Dostoyevsky, who "felt ideas" and who made them so splendidly individual! Chekhov did not "feel ideas," and when his characters give expression to theirs, they speak a colorless and monotonous journalese. *The Duel* is especially disfigured by such harangues. This is perhaps Chekhov's tribute to a deep-rooted tradition of Russian intelligentsia literature. Their speeches may have had some emotional significance in their time but certainly have none today. Another serious shortcoming is Chekhov's Russian. It is colorless and lacks individuality. He had no feeling for words. No Russian writer of anything like his significance used a language so devoid of all raciness and nerve. This makes Chekhov (except for topical allusions, technical terms, and occasional catch-words) so easy to translate. Of all Russian writers, he has the least to fear from the treachery of translators.

Chekhov's direct influence on Russian literature was not important. The success of his short stories contributed to the great popularity of that form, which became the predominant form in Russian fiction. But Gorky, Kuprin, and Bunin, to name but the foremost of those who regarded him as their master, can hardly be recognized as his pupils. Certainly no one learned from him the art of constructing his stories. His dramas, which looked so easy to imitate, were imitated, but the style proved a pitfall. Today[5] Russian fiction is quite free from any trace of Chekhov's influence. Some of the younger writers began, before the Revolution, as his more or less unintelligent imitators, but none of them remained true to him. In Russia, Chekhov has become a thing of the past—of a past remoter than even Turgenev, not to speak of Gogol or Leskov. Abroad, things stand differently. If Chekhov has had a genuine heir to the secrets of his art, it is in England, where Katherine Mansfield did what no Russian has done—learned from Chekhov without imitating him. In England, and to a lesser degree in France, the cult of Chekhov has become the hallmark of the highbrow intellectual. Curiously enough, in Russia, Chekhov was always regarded as a distinctly "lowbrow" writer; the self-conscious intellectual elite was always conspicuously cool to him. The highbrows of the beginning of the century even affected to (or sincerely did) despise him. His real stronghold was in the heart of the honest Philistine in the street. Nowadays Chekhov has of course become the common property of the nation. His place as a classic—a major classic, one of the "ten best"—is not challenged. But he is a classic who has been temporarily shelved.

NOTES

* From D. S. Mirsky, *A History of Russian Literature* (New York: Knopf, 1949), Vol. II, pp. 353–67. This essay originally appeared in 1926. Titles of stories in the critical essays conform to those in this collection, but quotations may differ.

1. A great inconvenience of the English edition of *Chekhov* is that it entirely disregards dates and arranges the tales in an arbitrary order. [Mirsky refers to the edition in thirteen volumes translated by Constance Garnett.—*Editor.*]

2. Tolstoy is said to have held this story in high esteem, and one cannot help noticing a certain similarity it bears to his own masterpiece *Alyosha Gorshok*, written eighteen years later.

3. *Letters of Anton Tchehov*, translated by Constance Garnett (London: Chatto & Windus, 19200, p. 101.

4. *The Wife and Other Stories*, translated by Constance Garnett (New York: 1916–22), pp. 218–19.

5. Mirsky's essay was first published in 1926. Even then his comments must have seemed outrageously opinionated. Chekhov's stories retain their popularity in Russia as elsewhere. [*Editor.*]

Chronology

1860	Born January 17 in Taganrog, small port on the sea of Azov in the Crimea.
1869	Admitted to local *gimnaziya* (combined grammar and high school).
1875	Father, a grocer, goes bankrupt and flees to Moscow.
1876	Family evicted from home. All go to Moscow except Anton, who remains in Taganrog to finish high school.
1879	Joins family in Moscow and enrolls in Medical Department of University of Moscow.
1880–84	Begins contributing humorous sketches and short stories to magazines under pen name Antosha Chekhonte.
1884	Begins medical practice in Moscow. First collection of short stories published.
1886	Starts contributing to *New Times*. Becomes lifelong friend of Alexei Suvorin, its millionaire owner.
1887	His play *Ivanov* performed in Moscow to a mixture of hissing and clapping. Two collections of short stories published.
1888	Writes four one-act "vaudevilles" for the theater. Long tale "The Steppe" receives high praise. Awarded Pushkin Prize for Literature by the Academy of Sciences.

1890	Travels to Sakhalin Island in Siberia to study penal colony.
1891	Travels with Suvorin to Western Europe, visiting Vienna, Venice, Rome, and Paris.
1892	Buys an estate near village of Melikhovo. Helps organize relief for famine victims. Organizes medical relief for cholera epidemic.
1894	Begins work on three schools he builds in Melikhovo area.
1895	Visits Tolstoy at Yasnaya Polyana. They become lifelong friends. *Island of Sakhalin* published.
1896	*The Seagull*: opening night a fiasco.
1897	Suffers violent lung hemorrhage. Winters in Nice, France.
1898	Settles in suburb of Yalta. First performance of *The Seagull* by Moscow Art Theater an immense success.
1899	Sells rights to all his works (except plays) to publisher A. F. Marx for 75,000 rubles. *Uncle Vanya* premieres at Moscow Art Theater.
1900	Marries actress Olga Knipper. Premiere of *The Three Sisters* at Moscow Art Theater.
1901–02	Health continues to deteriorate. Working on *The Cherry Orchard*.
1904	*The Cherry Orchard* premieres on January 17, in honor of Chekhov's birthday and twenty-five years of literary endeavor. Goes with Olga to German health resort of Badenweiler. Dies there on July 2.

Works by Anton Chekhov

The Tales of Melpomene, 1884
Motley Stories, 1886
In the Twilight, 1887
"The Kiss," 1887
Innocent Tales, 1887
Ivanov, 1887
The Steppe, 1888
"The Name-Day Party," 1888
The Bear, 1888
Stories, 1889
The Proposal, 1889
The Wedding, 1890
The Anniversary, 1891
"Ward Six," 1892
Sakhalin Island, 1893-95
"The Black Monk," 1894
The Seagull, 1896
"Peasants," 1897
Uncle Vanya, 1897
"In the Ravine," 1900
The Three Sisters, 1901
"The Bride," 1903
The Cherry Orchard, 1904

Works about Anton Chekhov

Avilova, Lydia. *Chekhov in My Life*, London: 1950.

Benedetti, Jean. *Dear Writer, Dear Actress:The Love Letters of Anton Chekhov and Olga Knipper*. Hopewell, New Jersey: Ecco Press, 1996.

Bruford, W. H. *Anton Chekhov*. Studies in Modern Literature and Thought. New Haven: Yale University Press, 1957.

Bristow, Eugene, ed. *Anton Chekhov's Plays.* New York: W. W. Norton & Co., 1977.

Callow, Phillip. *Chekhov: The Hidden Ground.* Chicago: Ivan R. Dee, 1998.

Chertok, I. C. and Jean Gardner, trans. *Late Blooming Flowers*. New York: McGraw-Hill Co., 1964.

Constantine, Peter, trans. *Forty-Three New Stories*. New York: Seven Stories Press, 1998.

Dunnigan, Ann, trans. *Chekhov: The Major Plays*. New York: Penguin Books, 1982.

Emaljanow, Victor, ed. *Chekhov: The Critical Heritage. London:* Routledge & Kegan Paul, 1981.

Fen, Elisaveta, trans. *Anton Chekhov Plays*. New York: Penguin Books, 1951.

Ford, Richard, ed. *The Essential Tales of Chekhov*. Hopewell, New Jersey: Ecco Press, 1998.

Frayn, Michael, trans. *Chekhov Plays*. London: Methuen Publishing Ltd., 1988.

Gorky, Maxim. (Katherine Mansfield, S.S. Koteliansky, and Leonard Woolf, trans.). *Reminiscences of Tolstoy, Chekhov, and Andreev*,.London: 1968. First published 1921.

Hingley, Ronald. *Chekhov: A Biographical and Critical Study*. London: Allen & Unwin, 1966.

———. *A New Life of Anton Chekhov*. New York: Alfred A. Knopf, 1976.

Jackson, Robert Louis, ed. *Chekhov: A Collection of Critical Essays*. Englewood Cliffs, N.J.: Prentice-Hall, 1967.

Karlinsky, Simon, ed. *Anton Chekhov's Life and Thought: Selected Letters and Commentary*. Henry Heim and Simon Karlinsky, trans. Evanston, Ill.: Northwestern U. Press, 1999.

Kolteliansky, S.S. and Leonard Woolf (trans.). *Notebook of Anton Chekhov*. Hopewell, NJ: Ecco Press, 1987. First published 1921.

Kulka, John, ed. *The Best Stories of Anton Chekhov*. New York: Barnes & Noble, 2000.

Lafitte, Sophie. *Chekhov: 1860-1904*. New York: Charles Scribner's Sons, 1971.

Llewellyn Smith, Virginia. *Anton Chekhov and the Lady with the Dog*. Oxford: Oxford University Press, 1973.

Margarshack, David. *Chekhov the Dramatist*. New York: Hill & Wang, 1960.

———. *The Real Chekhov*. New York: Barnes & Noble Books, 1973.

Payne, Robert, trans. *The Image of Chekhov: Forty Stories by Anton Chekhov*. New York: Alfred A. Knopf, 1963.

Pritchett, V. S. *Chekhov: A Spirit Set Free*. New York: Random House, 1988.

Rayfield, Donald. *Anton Chekhov: A Life*. New York: Henry Holt & Co, 1997.

———. *Chekhov: The Evolution of His Art*. New York: Barnes & Noble, 1975.

Schmidt, Paul, trans. *The Plays of Anton Chekhov*. New York, Harper Collins, 1997.

Simmons, Ernest J. *Chekhov: A Biography*. Boston: Little Brown & Co., 1962.

Terpak, Luba and Michael Terpak, trans. *The Island: A Journey to Sakhalin*. New York: Washington Square Press, 1967.

Troyat, Henri. *Chekhov*. New York: Ballantine Books, 1988.

Wilson, Edmund, ed. *Peasants and Other Stories*. New York: New York Review of Books, 1999.

Yarmolinsky, Avrahm, ed. *The Portable Chekhov*. New York: Viking Press, 1968.

WEBSITES

Anton Chekhov – the Definitive Site
www.geocities.com/Athens/Forum/1702/index.html

The Chekhov Papers
www.ups.edu/professionalorgs/dramaturgy/seagull/chekpap.htm

International Chekhov's Fund
www.chekhov.org

Literature, Arts, and Medicine Database – Anton P. Chekhov
endeavor.med.nyu.edu/lit-med/lit-med-db/webdocs/webauthors/chekhov68-au-.html

Nebraska Center for Writers
mockingbird.creighton.edu/NCW/chekhov.htm

Taganrog Central
lynx.dac.neu.edu/a/amakhank/taganrog/

Top-Biography—Anton Chekhov
www.top-biography.com/9143-Anton%20Chekhov/

Contributors

HAROLD BLOOM is Sterling Professor of the Humanities at Yale University and Henry W. and Albert A. Berg Professor of English at the New York University Graduate School. He is the author of over 20 books, including *Shelley's Mythmaking* (1959), *The Visionary Company* (1961), *Blake's Apocalypse* (1963), *Yeats* (1970), *A Map of Misreading* (1975), *Kabbalah and Criticism* (1975), *Agon: Toward a Theory of Revisionism* (1982), *The American Religion* (1992), *The Western Canon* (1994), and *Omens of Millennium: The Gnosis of Angels, Dreams, and Resurrection* (1996). *The Anxiety of Influence* (1973) sets forth Professor Bloom's provocative theory of the literary relationships between the great writers and their predecessors. His most recent books include *Shakespeare: The Invention of the Human*, a 1998 National Book Award finalist, and *How to Read and Why*, which was published in 2000. In 1999, Professor Bloom received the prestigious American Academy of Arts and Letters Gold Medal for Criticism.

ELIZABETH SILVERTHORNE is a freelance writer from Texas, and has written extensively on Texas history. Her other works include biographies on Sarah Orne Jewett and Majorie Kinnan Rawlings.

VIRGINIA LLEWELLYN SMITH has written on Chekhov and Henry James. Her works include *Anton Chekhov and the Lady with the Dog* (1973), *Henry James and the Real Thing: A Modern Reader* (1994), and most recently, she edited and introduced *The Golden Bowl* by Henry James (1999).

EDMUND WILSON was an essayist, political thinker, journalist, novelist, and playwright. After graduating from Princeton, Wilson began his career as an editor of Vanity Fair and the New Republic. *Axel's Castle*, one of his earliest achievements and a study of Symbolism, is still well-regarded. As an essayist, he tackled literature, history, politics, and travel—a range demonstrated in the countless collections of his work, which include *Scrolls from the Dead Sea*, *Patriotic Gore*, *Europe without Baedecker*, and *A Window on Russia*, which is considered to be one of the most stimulating introductions to the Russian greats—Tolstoy, Pushkin, Gogol, Chekhov. Excerpts from his diary live on in *The Twenties*, considered to be one of the most seminal portraits of an age. His fiction includes the novel *I Thought of Daisy* and the short story collection *Memoirs of Hectate County*. Wilson's correspondences are legendary; perhaps the most well-known epistolary relationship was with Vladamir Nabokov.

D. S. MIRSKY was a Russian literary critic, whose enormous *History of Russian Literature* (1926-1927) remains uncontested in its greatness. Born Prince Dimitry Patrovich Svytopolk-Mirsky into one of the oldest Russian princely families, Mirsky lived much of his life in Britain after the revolution of 1905. There, he made the acquaintance of T. S. Eliot, Aldous Huxley, Bertrand Russell, and Leonard and Virginia Woolf. It was also in London that Mirsky published the majority of his work, including the aforementioned *History*, as well as biographies on Pushkin and Lenin, several anthologies of Russian literature, and two histories. Mirsky returned to the Soviet Union in 1932, where he managed to live and write for another few years before being arrested and dying in a prison camp on June 6, 1939.

INDEX